Above: Tresaith
Front cover: Mwnt
Back cover: Aberystwyth

Written by: Miles Cowsill

Revised and updated by: Trevor Barrett

Photography: Wales Tourist Board,
Lily Publications

First published
by Lily Publications 1994

Second (revised) edition 1995

Third (revised) edition 1997

Fourth (revised) edition 1999

Copyright © 1999 Lily Publications. All rights reserved. Any reproduction in whole or in part is strictly prohibited. The content contained herein is based on the best available information at the time of research. The publishers assume no liability whatsoever arising from the publishing of material contained herein.

All accommodation advertised in this guide participates in the Wales Tourist Board's inspection scheme. If readers have any concern about the standards of any accommodation, please take the matter up directly with the provider of the accommodation, as soon as possible. Failing satisfaction, please contact the Wales Tourist Board, Development Services Unit, Brunel House, 2 Fitzalan Road, Cardiff CF2 1UY.

Published by Lily Publications, PO Box 9, Narberth, Pembrokeshire, Wales SA68 0YT.
Tel: (01834) 891461, Fax: (01834) 891463.
ISBN 1 899602 550.

Contents

A Unique Guide to Cardiganshire 4
A Land Shaped by the Sea 5
The Great Beach Holiday..8
Your A-Z of Cardiganshire...16
The Great Sporting & Activity Holiday 60
Guardian of a Nation's Heritage - *the National Library of Wales*................67
Exploring North & South of Cardiganshire....................................69
Index 80

Maps

Cardiganshire..14/15
Aberaeron..16   Cardigan...32
Aberystwyth..23   New Quay.....................................51

Llangrannog

Quay West
New Quay, West Wales

- ✦ Brilliant Family Holiday Park
- ✦ Heated Indoor and Outdoor Pool
- ✦ Bradley Bear Kids Club
- ✦ Tennis Courts, Pitch and Putt
- ✦ Crazy Golf, Multi Sports Courts
- ✦ Amusements
- ✦ SplashZone, FunWorks
- ✦ Sparkling Family Cabaret
- ✦ Bars, Discos, Bingo and Karaoke
- ✦ Great Food Available
- ✦ Holiday Homes Sleeping 2-8
- ✦ Plus Much, Much More

Call now to book and to claim your free colour brochure

LO CALL 0345 422 422

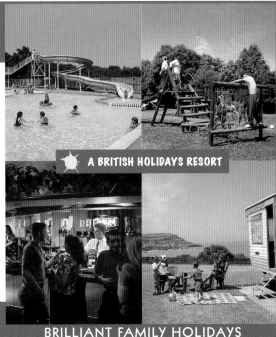

A BRITISH HOLIDAYS RESORT

BRILLIANT FAMILY HOLIDAYS

We have customers from all over Britain ...this is why!

- ● The largest choice of modern, traditional and reproduction furniture anywhere in Wales.
- ● All our products are competitively priced and include FREE delivery in England and Wales.
- ● We offer traditional customer service that only an independent company can provide.

HAFREN FURNISHERS

LLANIDLOES, POWYS. TEL: (01686) 412137
Open Mon-Sat, 9am-6pm Late night Thursday 8pm
Why not telephone for further information without obligation

Famous brand names for less
Including: Ercol, Parker Knoll, Nathan, G-Plan, Stag, Alstons, Jaycee, Myers, Rest
Assured, Dunlopillo, Staples, Slumberland, Morris, Ducal and Old Charm

FREE PARKING ● IN HOUSE CAFETERIA ● JUST OFF THE A470

3

Croeso · Bienvenue
Welkom · Willkommen

CROESO

Mae hi yn wastad yn bleser cael croesawu ymwelwyr o rannau eraill o Gymru, a rydym yn hyderus y bydd y llawlyfr hwn o gymorth i chi i wneud y gorau o'ch gwyliau.

Mae'r gyfrol hon yn un o gyfres lwyddiannus *Premier Guides* a gyhoeddir gan wasg leol Lily Publications, a chaiff ei diweddaru'n gyson er mwyn cadw'r wybodaeth sydd ynddi mor gywir a chyfredol â phosib.

Hwn yw'r llawlyfr mwya cynhwysfawr y gallwch ei brynu ar gyfer y rhan hon o Gymru, gan ddod ynghyd, o fewn cloriau un llyfryn hawdd-ei-ddarllen, fanylion am lu o atyniadau naturiol ac o waith dyn. Mae'r rhain yn amrywio o harddwch cefn gwlad i gestyll o'r Oesoedd Canol, trefi a phentrefi o ddiddordeb hanesyddol arbennig, amgueddfeydd, gweithgareddau chwaraeon a hamdden, adloniant, bywyd gwyllt, gwyliau a digwyddiadau, a llawer llawer mwy.

Gallwch gadarnhau manylion agor, prisau mynediad ac ati yn uniongyrchol gyda'r atyniadau unigol (mae eu rhifau ffôn yn cael eu rhestru yn y llawlyfr) neu gyda'r Canolfannau Croeso lleol (sydd hefyd yn cael eu nodi).

Yn olaf, rydym yn sicr y gwnewch chi gytuno bod y canllaw hwn yn werth pob dimau. Felly mwynhewch ei ddarllen, a chofiwch gael gwyliau bythgofiadwy a fydd wrth eich bodd.

BIENVENUE

C'est toujours pour moi un immense plaisir d'accueillir des visiteurs dont la langue maternelle n'est pas l'anglais et nous espérons sincèrement que ce guide vous permettra de profiter au maximum de vos vacances. Faisant partie d'une série primée de *Premier Guides*, publiée par la maison d'édition locale Lily Publications, ce volume est mis à jour régulièrement dans le but de garder les informations qui y sont contenues aussi précises et actualisées que possible.

Il s'agit également du guide le plus complet de cette région du Pays de Galles vendu sur le marché, car il donne des renseignements pratiques sur une multitude de choses à faire et d'endroits à visiter, construits soit par la nature soit par la main de l'homme. Ces lieux de visite varient de la beauté du paysage de châteaux, de villes et de villages qui présentent un intérêt historique considérable, à des musées, des centres de sports et de loisirs, des lieux de divertissement, des parcs naturels, des festivals et autres spectacles et bien plus encore.

Des renseignements concernant les heures d'ouverture, les tarifs d'entrée et autres renseignements pratiques sont indiqués pour chaque lieu de visite (des numéros de téléphone sont donnés dans toute la brochure) ou dans les Centres d'Information Tourisme (qui sont également listés dans ce fascicule).

Nous sommes convaincus que vous trouverez ce guide indispensable et extrêmement complet pour son prix. Bonne lecture et passez des vacances inoubliables.

WELKOM

Het is altijd een eer om bezoekers welkom te heten die een andere taal dan het Engels spreken. We hopen van harte dat deze gids zal bijdragen aan een heerlijke vakantie.

Dit boek maakt deel uit van de serie *Premier Guides*, bestsellers uitgebracht door Lily Publications. Het wordt regelmatig herzien met als doel de opgenomen informatie zo accuraat en actueel mogelijk te houden.

Het is tevens de meest uitgebreide gids voor dit deel van Wales die er te koop is. Het brengt op eenvoudige wijze en in één band gegevens samen over een hele verzameling natuur- en door de mens gemaakte attracties. Deze variëren van de pracht van het landschap tot middeleeuwse kastelen, steden en dorpjes van groot geschiedkundig belang, musea, sport- en ontspanningsactiviteiten, amusement, natuur, festivals en evenementen, en nog veel meer.

Gegevens betreffende openingstijden, toegangsprijzen, enzovoorts kunnen rechtstreeks bij de individuele attracties (telefoonnummers in deze gids) of bij een plaatselijk Tourist Information Centre (Brits VVV-kantoor) (tevens in deze gids vermeld) worden nagegaan.

Tenslotte vertrouwen we erop dat u het met ons eens zal zijn dat deze gids zijn geld meer dan waard is. Dus veel plezier bij het lezen - en een plezierige en gedenkwaardige vakantie toegewenst.

WILLKOMMEN

Es ist uns immer eine große Freude, Besucher, deren Muttersprache nicht Englisch ist, willkommen zu heißen, und wir hoffen sehr, daß dieser Führer dazu beiträgt, das meiste aus Ihren Ferien zu machen.

Dieser Band aus der Reihe der bestverkauften Premier Guides des lokalen Unternehmens Lily Publications wird regelmäßig aktualisiert, um die darin enthaltenen Informationen so genau und so aktuell wie möglich zu halten.

Auch handelt es sich hierbei um wohl den umfassendsten Führer dieser Gegend von Wales, den Sie kaufen können und in welchem die Angaben zu der Unmenge an sowohl landschaftlichen als auch von Menschenhand geschaffenen Sehenswürdigkeiten in einem leicht zu lesendem Buch zusammengefaßt sind. Diese reichen von prächtigen Landschaften bis hin zu mittelalterlichen Schlössern, Städten und Dörfern von großem historischem Interesse, Museen, Sport und Freizeitaktivitäten, Unterhaltung, Tieren auf freier Wildbahn, Festivals und Veranstaltungen und daneben noch vieles mehr.

Genaue Angaben zu Öffnungszeiten, Eintrittsgebühren u.s.w. können direkt mit den einzelnen Attraktionen (Telefonnummern sind im Führer angegeben) oder mit den örtlichen Fremdenverkehrsämtern (die Sie hier ebenfalls aufgelistet finden) verglichen werden.

Wir sind davon überzeugt, daß Sie mit uns einer Meinung sein werden, dieser Führer ist sein Geld wert. Wir wünschen Ihnen viel Spaß beim Lesen - und einen angenehmen und unvergeßlichen Aufenthalt.

4

C eredigion, or Cardiganshire, is best known for its spectacular coastline, glorious beaches and ever-popular resorts.

Yet the county has many other faces, and away from the coast it is as wild, varied and breathtaking as Wales itself. The lonely hills of Plynlimon - the highest point of central Wales - and the vast peat bog of Tregaron are as different from the coastal plateau of Cardigan Bay as any landscape designer could conceive. Similarly, if you stand among the bustle and banter of Lampeter's livestock market, or follow in the tracks of the old drovers across the Abergwesyn Pass, the county's golden beaches could be a million miles away. More enchanting still is that Ceredigion is virtually an island. Not only is it bounded on three sides by water - Cardigan Bay to the west, the River Dovey to the north and the River Teifi to the south; it is also 'cut off' on its eastern border by the Cambrian Mountains.

A land shaped by the sea

And like an island, Ceredigion is very individual in character and even has its own capital - Aberystwyth. It also has a history of seafaring, shipbuilding and smuggling, and a long tradition of digging for treasure; lead, silver and gold have all been very actively mined in the county at one time or another.

The Cardis (as the natives of Ceredigion are called) are to a greater extent Welsh speaking, particularly around the market towns of the Teifi Valley, and are fiercely

Llangrannog

proud of their Celtic heritage and traditions, and of the Welsh language. The first National Eisteddfod - Wales' great annual festival of poetry and music - was held in Cardigan in the 12th century. Much earlier, Celtic saints had passed this way on their pilgrimage to Bardsey Island, and churches all along the coast are dedicated to them. And while the clanging of the shipwright's hammer and the clamour of the mines are long silent, in Ceredigion today coracles are still fishing, waterwheels are still turning, woollen mills are still weaving and steam trains are still running.

These strong links with the past have helped to present visitors with a rich selection of things to do and places to see - some of them totally unexpected, and all the more pleasurable for that.

Equally, Ceredigion sports many outstanding locations and facilities for golfers, sailors, windsurfers and anglers. This is also ideal pony trekking country, while the week-long Ian Rush International Soccer Tournament in Aberystwyth is the biggest event of its kind in Europe, attracting some of the greatest soccer clubs in world football as both boys' and girls' teams battle for honours.

The Heritage Coast Anyone who knows the beaches of Clarach, New Quay, Tresaith, Llangrannog and Mwnt - to name but a few - also knows that the Ceredigion coastline is characterised by magnificent cliff scenery. In 1982, this was officially recognised when four sections, totalling 22 miles in length, were designated Heritage Coast.

Such a designation is not rare in Britain, but it does acknowledge that these particular stretches of Ceredigion coastline are of special interest and value and their landscape merits protection. Altogether there are 900 miles - 44 sections - of English and Welsh Heritage Coast. By definition they are spectacular, undeveloped and highly varied, ranging from salt marshes to high cliffs, headlands to long isolated stretches.

Ceredigion's four sections of Heritage Coast lie between the following locations: Gwbert-on-Sea and Pen-peles; Tresaith and New Quay; Llanrhystud and Monk's Cave; and Clarach and Borth.

The Marine Heritage Coast In the fight against pollution and to help conserve the region's natural resources, Ceredigion District Council is now working hard to establish a Marine Heritage Coast in the section between Tresaith and New Quay.

This will encompass not only the shoreline and many cliff nesting sites of seabirds, but also a mile-wide corridor of sea which is a haven for marine wildlife such as bottle-nosed dolphins, harbour porpoises and grey seals. Locals, visitors and wildlife will all benefit from this initiative, and particularly those who use Cardigan Bay for leisure and recreation.

Living off the Sea Historically the hamlets, villages and towns of Ceredigion have managed to eke out a living from the land and the sea for generation after generation, and at least 40,000 of the county's 60,000 population still live along the coast.

In the past, the open coastal plains around Aberaeron and Llansantffraid - known as the barley belt - were big grain producers, while others depended on mixed farming. Often, agriculture was supplemented by fishing. For many communities this was done on a modest scale - either from the shore or in small boats - but places like Aberaeron, New Quay and Aberystwyth developed substantial fishing fleets. At one time Aberystwyth was the most important herring port in Wales. One night in 1745 the 47 boats working from the port landed one and a quarter million herring.

Sea trade along the western seaways, which probably originated in the Iron Age,

Mwnt

was booming by the 19th century. During this period the economy of Cardigan Bay was sustained by a diet of fish and ships as shipbuilding became big business. Small coastal trading vessels were in great demand and could be built virtually anywhere, with shipyards springing up in the unlikeliest places along the shoreline. Llangrannog, Llanina Point, Aberarth, Llanon and Llanrhystud were all thriving centres of a prosperous industry - in addition to the major yards of Cardigan, New Quay, Aberaeron and Aberystwyth.

A Smugglers' Paradise A coastline riddled with secluded coves and secret caves provided free warehousing for smugglers in the 18th century. The area around New Quay was particularly well endowed with such hideouts, and illicit trade was so rife here that in 1795 New Quay was described by the authorities as a place of "infamous notoriety".

The contraband included such desirable goods as French brandy, tobacco, tea, wines and salt. Brandy and tobacco returned the biggest profits and came ashore mainly at the hands of French smugglers, to be disposed of in Lampeter and Tregaron. No doubt the drovers who passed through these market towns were easily persuaded to prepare for the long trek to the markets of England by downing a cut-price tot or two of best French liquor. Among the places most associated with smuggling along the Ceredigion coastline were Cwmtydu, which was also a favourite haunt of pirates, and beautiful Penbryn, which became known as Smugglers' Valley.

This Way for a Great Holiday Sea trade and shipbuilding continued to flourish along the Ceredigion coast well into the late 19th century. But gradually the old vessels of wood and sail were replaced by bigger and faster ships of iron and steam, quickly followed by the advent of road and rail transport - changes which dealt the death blow to Cardigan Bay's short-lived prosperity.

But it was not all bad news, because the railways brought with them an exciting and challenging new industry to the region - tourism. An industry which has continued to grow, and is now one of the mainstays of Ceredigion's economy.

7

The Great Beach Holiday

Aberaeron South Beach(Traeth Y De)
Aberporth (Dyffryn & Dolwen
Aberystwyth North (Traeth Y Gogledd)
Aberystwyth South Beach (Traeth Y De)
Borth
Cilborth (Llangrannog)
Clarach
Cwmtydu
Llangrannog
Llanrhystud
Mwnt
New Quay (Traeth Harbwr)
New Quay (Traeth Y Dolau)
New Quay (Traethgwyn)
Penbryn
Tresaith

*Your quick-reference guide to
Ceredigion's beaches*

W ith its popular resorts and many fine beaches, the Ceredigion coastline is a natural attraction for those in search of a traditional seaside holiday. It is also a major draw for sailing and watersport enthusiasts, anglers, walkers, birdwatchers, photographers, artists and many others with special interests. And in 1998 no less than 16 of Ceredigion's beaches qualified for the Tidy Britain Group's Seaside Award - a UK award scheme encompassing both resort and rural beaches. Its primary functions are to help raise standards of cleanliness, hygiene, safety and environmental management at beaches, and also to provide a comprehensive and free information service for all beach users.

The scheme is administered by the Tidy Britain Group, an independent national charity. The Ceredigion beaches granted a Seaside Award in 1996 are listed here in alphabetical order.

The following guide describes the county's beaches in order of location, from Ynyslas in the north to Mwnt in the south.

Ynyslas Reaching right into the mouth of the beautiful Dovey (Dyfi) estuary, Ynyslas has an expansive sandy foreshore and a mass of sand dunes which are part of the Dyfi National Nature Reserve. Bathing here is unsafe because of the treacherous estuary currents, but this is nevertheless one of the most popular natural beauty spots in Ceredigion - a sanctuary for anyone who values the freedom of wide open spaces, and a refuge for waders, wildfowl and butterflies. Across the estuary is the resort of Aberdovey, and in the distance are the hills of Plynlimon and the Snowdonia National Park, with seaward views of Strumble Head and the Lleyn Peninsular. Ynyslas also has a Wildlife Information Centre.

Borth There's no doubting Borth's main attraction: its superb 4-mile beach of clean, unbroken sand, which extends seawards for about 150 yards at low tide and northwards

Ynyslas

Borth

flatfish are the most common catches. Low tide gives access to rock pools which extend around the base of the cliffs. The cliffs between Upper Borth and Clarach mark the most northerly section of the Ceredigion Heritage Coast. In 1998 Borth won a Seaside Award from the Tidy Britain Group.

Clarach Clarach beach lies in the shelter of steep shale cliffs, along which magnificent coastal walks extend in both directions - Borth to the north and Aberystwyth to the south. At low tide larger areas of sand become exposed, studded with rocky outcrops. There are also rocky platforms extending on either side of the bay, creating rock pools at low tide. In 1998 Clarach won a Seaside Award from the Tidy Britain Group.

Aberystwyth Aberystwyth's North Beach is a gently sloping beach of sand and shingle. The bay in which it sits enjoys a fair degree of shelter, as the foothills of the Cambrian Mountains rise behind the town. The beach also has the benefit of being close to the

to Ynyslas and the Dovey estuary. The water is shallow and safe for bathing (except around Ynyslas and the estuary). Borth is much favoured by windsurfers and surfers, and there is a designated area for sand yachting and a slipway for small sailing craft. The northern end of the village boasts a promenade, with benches overlooking the beach. Sea angling is popular here; bass and

Aberystwyth

many shops, restaurants and other services and facilities which have helped establish Aberystwyth as the biggest seaside resort in West Wales. In 1998 the North Beach won a Seaside Award from the Tidy Britain Group.

Tan-y-bwlch Serving as Aberystwyth's south beach, Tan-y-bwlch is considered to be the best shingle-and-sand beach in Ceredigion, and is home to a distinctive plant community. A mile and a half long, the beach is immediately south of Aberystwyth harbour and is popular for walking. However, strong offshore currents make bathing dangerous. Behind the beach is the Ystwyth valley, on one side of which are the steep slopes of Pen Dinas - the site of an Iron Age hillfort. In 1998 Tan-Y-Bwlch won a Seaside Award from the Tidy Britain Group.

Llanrhystud Llanrhystud lies along the banks of the River Wyre, a mile from the sea, and its two spacious beaches offer a variety of scenery. They are contained in the gentle curve between the low headland at Llansantffraid and the stack of Carreg Ti-pw. The main beach is composed of boulders and pebbles, but during low water wide strips of flat sand are exposed. To the south is the second beach, where shipbuilding once thrived, and throughout the last century the four kilns at nearby Craiglas were the scene of a prosperous lime industry. There are also many rock pools to explore here. From Llanryhstud, the cliffs extending north to Monk's Cave are designated Heritage Coast. In 1998 Llanrhystud won a Seaside Award from the Tidy Britain Group.

Llansantffraid Llansantffraid is a quiet hamlet close to the village of Llanon. The beach is a mile long and composed of pebble and stone, with interesting rock pools and areas of sand exposed at low tide. The beach is backed by cliffs which mark the edge of the most extensive platform of boulder clay

along the Ceredigion coast. These cliffs, a favourite nesting site for sand martins, are being worn away by the continuous wave action of the sea.

Aberarth This small village is one mile north of Aberaeron, which can be reached along the foreshore. The beach consists of pebbles which have come from the cliffs of boulder clay and Aberystwyth Grits. At low tide, to the south of the village, you can see the remains of large, semi-circular stone walls. These were fish traps, designed to trap stranded fish such as salmon, sprats and mullet as the tide went out. Also of historic interest is the fact that hewn stones from Somerset were landed at Aberarth and then transported twelve miles overland for the building of Strata Florida Abbey.

Aberaeron Aberaeron's two beaches are composed mainly of stones and pebbles from the boulder clay on which the town is built. The southern beach is the more popular, since it has sandy areas and rock pools exposed at low tide. It also gives a superb view across the bay to New Quay.
In 1998 both of Aberaeron's south beach won a Seaside Award from the Tidy Britain Group.

Gilfach yr Halen This is a predominantly shingle-and-stone beach with a small amount of sand. It can be reached via an attractive coastal path from Aberaeron, and from the headland there are magnificent views northwards of the coast of Cardigan Bay.

Cei Bach Cei Bach is a peaceful and undeveloped sandy beach which lies within the mile-and-a-half sweep of Little Quay Bay, just east of New Quay. A narrow lane winds down to the beach, where the shallow waters are safe for bathing and a wide expanse of clean sand is exposed at low tide. Cei Bach is

New Quay

popular for windsurfing, surfing, canoeing and sailing, and there are scenic walks along the foreshore and the cliff tops towards Aberaeron.

New Quay New Quay is one of the most popular resorts along the Ceredigion coast. Set on the east-facing slopes of New Quay Head, it is sheltered from prevailing south-westerly winds by the 300-ft headland of Pencraig. In addition to the harbour beach, which is a crescent of sand offering safe bathing and boating facilities, New Quay has two other beaches. To the north is Traeth y Dolau, a predominantly stone beach backed by shale cliffs, and extending around New Quay Bay to the east is Traethgwyn, a gently-sloping shingle beach which at low tide becomes a vast expanse of clean golden sand. Traethgwyn is ideal for watersports, and with the tide out you can walk along the foreshore to Llanina Point and to sandy Cei Bach beach beyond. In the opposite direction, between New Quay Head and Tresaith,

stands the longest stretch of Ceredigion's four sections of Heritage Coast. In 1998 all three of New Quay's beaches won a Seaside Award from the Tidy Britain Group.

Cwmtydu Cwmtydu is a secluded cove to the south-west of New Quay, on the Heritage Coast. A predominantly shingle beach, it is enhanced at low tide by a small area of sand. An interesting feature is the large freshwater pool, popular with children, which is created by the action of storm waves throwing up pebbles and blocking the mouth of a stream. There are also shallow rock pools and dark caves to explore, and the folding and faulting in the cliffs clearly show how the rocks, once horizontal, have been subjected to tremendous earth-moving forces and are now vertical in places. A path near the beach takes you through National Trust property and overlooks the bay, and you might just be lucky enough to see basking seals and porpoises. In 1998 Cwmtydu won a Seaside Award from the Tidy Britain Group.

11

Llangrannog

Llangrannog Llangrannog lies in the narrow, steep-sided valley of the River Hawen. One of the most photographed and popular village resorts in West Wales, it is set amongst wonderful Heritage Coast scenery and has two fine sandy beaches: the main beach at its frontage, which has lifeguards on duty during the summer season and is popular for watersports, and Cilborth beach, a hidden cove accessible along the foreshore at low tide or via a descending cliff path. The appeal of the beaches is enhanced by walks along the Lochtyn Peninsular, owned by the National Trust, where you can enjoy spectacular views of the dramatic cliff scenery extending both north and south. In 1998 both Llangrannog and Cilborth beaches won a Seaside Award from the Tidy Britain Group.

Penbryn The ancient village of Penbryn is half a mile inland, set in a beautiful wooded valley. The beach, part of the Heritage Coast, is owned by the National Trust and is totally unspoilt. Three quarters of a mile long and consisting for the most part of fine golden sand, it is divided by a stream and backed by rocks and sand dunes.

This beach is a very popular spot in the summer, especially with children. Its shallow water also makes it one of the safest beaches in Cardigan Bay. At low tide you can walk along the foreshore to Tresaith. In 1998 Penbryn won a Seaside Award from the Tidy Britain Group.

Tresaith Popular Tresaith lies in a sheltered basin overlooking a beach of fine golden sands and shallow waters - one of the safest and most attractive beaches in West Wales, and part of the Heritage Coast. The retreating tide exposes a large area of sand and many rock pools. An unusual feature is

Penbryn

The beautiful coast of Cardigan Bay

the cascading waterfall formed by the River Saith as it tumbles over the cliffs to the east of the village. The beach also has a small slipway and boating is popular in summer. On a clear day the views from Tresaith are magnificent, but the cliffs which border the beach are a potential danger to children and great care should be taken. In 1998 Tresaith won a Seaside Award from the Tidy Britain Group.

Aberporth In a picturesque setting overlooking two sandy beaches, Aberporth is one of Ceredigion's most favoured village resorts. It is particularly popular with sailing enthusiasts and canoeists, and a slipway leads down to Dolwen Beach. Dyffryn Beach is ideal for beach games and the receding tide leaves plenty of rock pools to explore. Bathing in Aberporth's shallow waters is safe, except when the red warning flag is flying. In 1998 both Aberporth's Dyffryn & Dolwen Beach won a Seaside Award from the Tidy Britain Group.

Mwnt Mwnt is a remote sandy beach and headland, a few miles north of Cardigan, which is owned by the National Trust and part of Ceredigion's Heritage Coast. The clean golden beach is in an idyllic location, tucked inside a sheltered bay and protected from sea breezes - a natural sun trap. The rocks adjoining the beach are well patronised by fishermen hoping to land mackerel, bass, pollack and eels. This area is also a haven for seals, which can often be seen basking off the coast, particularly towards evening. In 1998 Mwnt won a Seaside Award from the Tidy Britain Group.

Mwnt

CARDIGAN

BAY

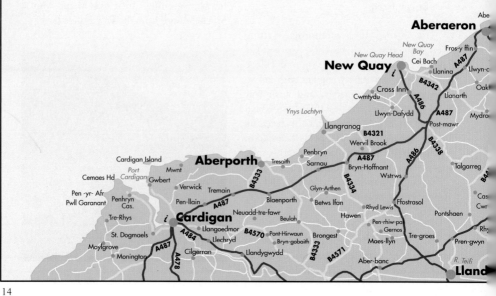

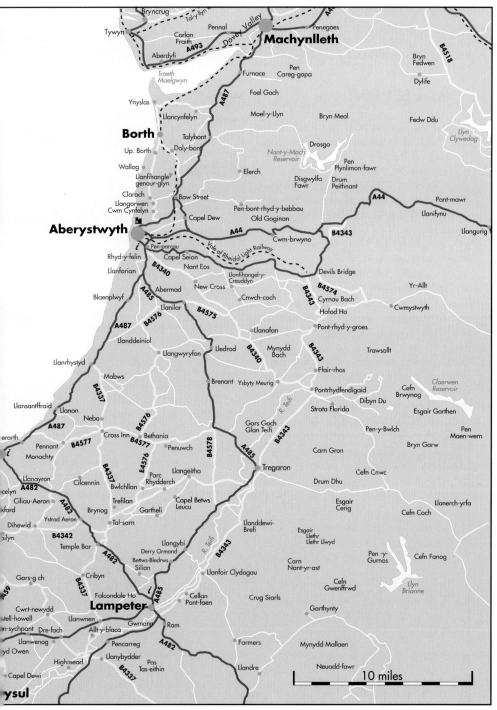

10 miles

15

The following is a quick-reference guide to the towns, villages and resorts of Ceredigion.

Aberaeron

Aberaeron

Aberaeron, a few miles up the bay from New Quay, lies on the low coastal platform at the mouth of the picturesque Aeron Valley. It is a very attractive and popular little town - a unique example of Regency town planning in Wales, with charming Georgian houses, squares and terraces, and a once-busy stone-walled harbour. Many of the town's buildings are designated as being of special or architectural interest.

The credit for the creation of this impressive resort goes to the Reverend Alban Thomas Jones Gwynne. In 1807 he was granted permission by an Act of Parliament to build two piers at the mouth of the River Aeron. So began a remarkable transformation. Aberaeron, at that time little more than a small group of houses clustered around a bridge, developed into a thriving port, where a flourishing shipbuilding industry and a large fleet of herring boats brought prosperity and prestige to the town on a scale beyond expectations.

Today Aberaeron nets more visitors than it does herring, and inevitably the place of the fishing boats has been taken by yachts and pleasure craft. The town has succeeded

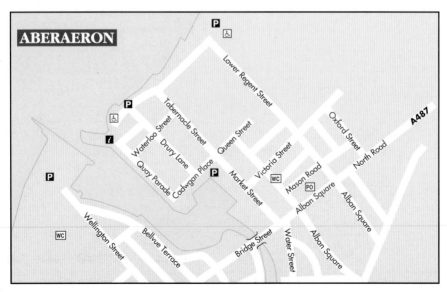

THE MONACHTY ARMS HOTEL

Overlooking the harbour in the centre of Aberaeron, this friendly, family-run hotel offers 8 rooms with TV, radio and drinks facilities (5 with en-suite facilities). Relax in warm comfortable surroundings in our restaurant or try the Hotel bar with a range of beers and hot/cold snacks. Other facilities include residents lounge, beer garden, launderette. Wales Tourist Board ✿✿✿ commended. Local attractions include three Golf Courses, Riding Stables, Strata Florida Abbey, Silver Mine, Butterfly Farm, Narrow Gauge Railway to Devil's Bridge, Funicular Railway to Camera Obscura.

The Monachty Arms Hotel, 7 Market Street, Aberaeron, Cardiganshire SA46 0AS. Telephone 01545 570389

FFYNNON LAS VINEYARD

Enjoy a stroll through a Welsh vineyard
See the scenery · Find that gift
Wine tasting included FREE in visit
Open Easter to September
Everyday from 2pm - 5pm
Other times/coach parties by appointment.
Lampeter Road, Aberaeron
Tel: 01545 570234

These include the Hive On the Quay honeybee exhibition and the National Trust and Tourist Information Centre, which is open all year round.

For day trippers, Aberaeron is a very convenient stopping place between Cardigan and Aberystwyth. But the resort has a great deal to offer in its own right, including two award-winning beaches, outstanding views over Cardigan Bay, superb coastal and countryside walks, and a good choice of value-for-money accommodation. A fine example of the latter is the Monachty Arms Hotel. Open to non-residents, and enjoying a lovely harbourside location, this relaxing and friendly establishment has been owned and managed by the same family since 1898 and has 8 bedrooms (5 of which enjoy en suite facilities) as well as a restaurant, two bars, cellar bistro and a beer garden.

Aberaeron Sea Aquarium The aquarium gives real insight into the marine life of Cardigan Bay's coastal waters and the traditional inshore fisheries on which the coastal communities were once so dependent. The variety of tanks contains local fish and shellfish, some species taken from rock pools and others from deep water, and the small lobster and fish hatcheries are intended to help restock local waters. There are ambitious plans to expand the lobster hatchery into a full-scale enterprise, achieving as many as 30,000 hatchings a year, and to help restock Cardigan Bay with other prime species such as scallops, prawns, dover sole, turbot and monkfish. The aquarium also has an absorbing large-screen video presentation of a fisherman's working life, past and present, showing boats at work in local waters and as far afield as Iceland and beyond. Other films on related subjects are also shown throughout the day. Upstairs there is a collection of photographs of old Aberaeron taken by Percy Lloyd on glass plates in the 19th century. Money-saving

admirably in retaining its grace and elegance, and is a very relaxing and enjoyable place to explore. This is due in no small measure to a great sense of civic pride; even the busiest part of the town - that which is dissected by the main A487 - is so neat and clean that the traffic has failed to make a detrimental impression, or to inject any urgency into the unhurried pace of life.

Several places of interest in Aberaeron merit a visit, particularly around the harbour.

ABERAERON SEA AQUARIUM

COASTAL VOYAGES

Discovering

CARDIGAN BAY'S MARINE ECOLOGY & HERITAGE COAST in a Unique boating experience

Tickets/Booking/ Information

ABERAERON SEA AQUARIUM

2 Quay Parade,Aberaeron,

**Ceredigion
SA46 0BT
TEL:01545 570142
FAX:01545 570160**

PLEASE BOOK IN ADVANCE. TELEPHONE BOOKINGS BY CREDIT CARD.

OPENING TIMES

10.00am-5.00pm Easter to Nov 1st
Ticket prices   Season Tickets
                    (4 tickets for price of 3)
Adult   £3.50   £10.50
Senior   £2.00   £6.00
Children £1.25   £3.75
Group price available on request.

18

Aberaeron

season tickets and group discounts are available. For more information ring 01545 570142.

Clos Penngarreg Courtyard This courtyard craft centre, only a minute from the town, is located in a beautiful setting and enjoys superb views over the bay. Formerly a farm, the attractive buildings have been sensitively converted into highly individual arts and crafts workshops and retail outlets, each of which offers an interesting selection of handmade items at direct-from-the-creator prices. You can also buy locally-produced food here. For more information ring 01545 571661 or 570460.

Derwen Welsh Cob Centre & Museum, Pennant, near Aberaeron The Welsh cob is a highly versatile breed, and the Centre has attracted orders for its horses from all over the world. It also attracts many visitors. You can see the cobs at work and play, and the museum gives an insight into how these impressive and sturdy animals have become synonymous with Welsh farming over the centuries. Pennant is a few miles due east of Aberaeron, accessible on the B4577 or via the B4337 at Llanon.

Gwinllan Ffynnon Las Vineyard You would hardly expect to find a vineyard braving the elements of the Ceredigion coastline! Yet the first wine was produced here in 1990 and is now supplied to local hotels and restaurants. Located in the

WOODLANDS CARAVAN PARK

Llanon, Nr Aberystwyth SY23 5LX

- AA ►►►/RAC approved park
- Caravan Club/Camping Club approved
- Small family run site. All facilities
- Personally supervised by owners

**Telephone Ian and Pat on -
01974 202342**

The Hive on the Quay•Aberaeron

- Famous Honey Ice Creams, Sorbets & Yoghurt Ices
- Honeybee Exhibition, antique honeypots and live bees in observation hives
- Egon Ronay starred restaurant in converted wharf overlooking the harbour selling seafood and chilled white wine, chowder, pâté, unusual salads, home-baked bread and cakes, special Honey Ice Cream concoctions, cream teas and espresso coffee
- Telephone **01545 570445** for various opening times.

beautiful Aeron Valley, on the outskirts of Aberaeron (A482 Aberaeron-Lampeter road), the vineyard has an acre of vines and offers guided and self-guided tours, with the chance to sample the refreshing, fruity tang of Ffynnon Las wine. For more information ring 01545 570234.

Honeybee Exhibition at The Hive on the Quay Standing on the Quay at Aberaeron is the converted coal wharf which houses the unique Honey Bee Exhibition. Winnie the Pooh would love this place! It is a novel and original visitor attraction which combines several ideas in one. In addition to the exhibition there is a specialist honey shop; a licensed cafe-restaurant which has achieved an annual star rating in Egon Ronay's guide for the last 16 years; and a shop selling a tempting selection of honey ice creams. The exhibition itself shows how honey bees and bumble bees live quite differently from each other. There is also a rare collection of antique honeypots. The honey shop sells everything from bears (of course!) to edible and cosmetic honey and beeswax polish and candles. For more information ring 01545 570445.

Aberarth

Aberarth is a small village just a mile up the coast from Aberaeron. It is one of the

Aberporth

earliest coastal settlements of Ceredigion, and the charm and character of its cottages is enhanced by the fact that local stone and beach pebbles were used in their construction. The beach itself consists of a variety of pebbles derived directly from the impressive boulder clay cliffs and the older cliffs of Aberystwyth Grits. The incessant pounding of the waves is undermining these cliffs, as shown by the notch which the sea has cut at their base. The cliffs here also bear other distinctive geological features. These give an indication of the earth-moving processes involved as the rocks were formed 400 million years ago, during the Silurian Era.

Aberarth nestles in a deep valley of the River Arth. The river boasts fast-flowing rapids, small waterfalls and deep pools, and is a big attraction for anglers. Also of interest to visitors is St. David's parish church, located on a hillside just south of Aberarth. Founded in the 6th century and rebuilt in 1860, the church has a 9th-century Celtic cross and three early-Christian inscribed stones from the 9th and 10th centuries.

Aberporth

This resort is centred around two compact and very popular sandy beaches. Sheltered from prevailing south-westerly winds, The invigorating sea air and shallow bay is an ideal boating and bathing area. Dyffryn Beach, the larger of the two, was the landing site for smacks, brigs, schooners and other trading vessels that supplied the village with goods in the 19th century; the rusty iron mooring rings that secured these ships can still be seen embedded in the rocks around the bay. Limekilns also stood near the beaches, supplying local farmers with lime for fertiliser, mortar and whitewash.

Aberporth was once famous for its herring. Attracted to the shallow waters in great numbers, they reputedly had a special flavour and were in great demand in the mining towns of South Wales. Towards the end of the 19th century, Aberporth began to attract the attention of holidaymakers, and the first regatta was held in 1909. The resort has never looked back, and today's visitors have a good choice of Wales Tourist Board-approved accommodation. One of the great delights of Aberporth is the exhilarating cliff-top walk to nearby Tresaith, the beach famous for its waterfall.

Aberystwyth

Aberystwyth is the largest town on the West Wales coast. and one of Wales's favourite traditional seaside resorts. There is evidence of a settlement here dating from 4000 BC and there was an Iron Age settlement on top of Pen Dinas, but the town was not established until the castle was built in 1277. It became a popular holiday destination with the coming of the railway in the 19th century, and Aberystwyth today performs a variety of important functions: seaside resort, cultural centre, university town, shopping centre and administrative centre. These differing roles, far from inducing an identity crisis, have given the town a distinct charm and character.

As a resort, Aberystwyth certainly has all the right credentials. Between the two headlands of Pen Dinas and Constitution Hill are the harbour, superb new marina, the ruins of the medieval castle, the pier, and the long curving promenade, whose impressive bow-windowed hotels and guest houses typify the town's wide choice of family-run accommodation. The beach here is shingle and sand and offers safe bathing. In the bustling town is a surprisingly good selection of shops, cafes, restaurants, attractions and amenities, including a first-class Tourist Information Centre.

Since 1872, Aberystwyth has also been an important university town. The building which marks this milestone in the resort's

*The*Welsh Black Inn

BOW STREET, ABERYSTWYTH
5 miles north of Aberystwyth

- En suite bedroom accommodation
- Felinfoel Welsh beers
- Restaurant a la carte menu
- Bar meals
- Welsh Black steaks
- Local produce
- Pool table
- Car park
- Beer garden
- Close to the sea

TEL 01970 828361

Bistro 33

**We are open
Monday to Saturday
10am Serving Coffee
& Light Meals all day
Lunch Specials are
12 - 2.30pm
Tea Garden
Evening Menu from 6pm**

North Parade, Aberystwyth,
Cardiganshire SY23 2JN
Tel: (01970) 615332

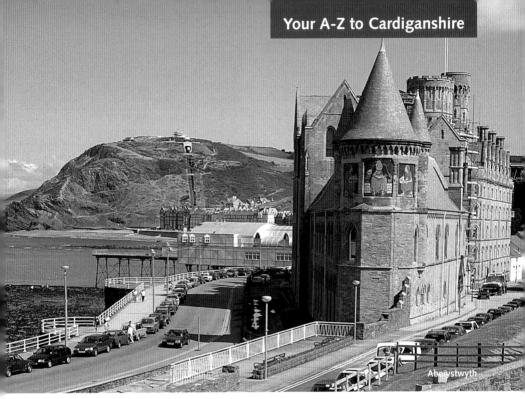

Aberystwyth

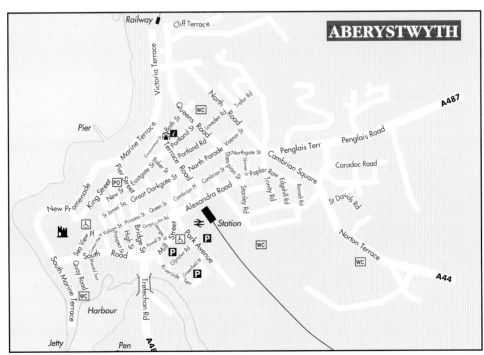

ABERYSTWYTH

Railway • Cliff Terrace

Victoria Terrace

North Road • Treflor Rd

A487

Queens Road • Loveden Rd

WC

Pier

Marine Terrace • Bath St • Portland St • Portland Rd • North Parade • Vaenor St • Northgate St • Penglais Terr • Penglais Road

Corporation St • Terrace Road • Cambrian Pl • Thespian St • Cambrian Square • Caradoc Road

Pier Street • Eastgate St • Baker St • Great Darkgate St • Poplar Row • Edgehill Rd • Bansdl Rd • St Davids Rd

King Street • New St

New Promenade • St James' Sq • Princess St • Queen St • Stanley Rd • Trinity Rd

Custom Hse St • Vulcan St • Alexandra Road

Sea View Pl • Prospect St • George St • Grays Inn Rd • ♦ Station

South Road • High St • Powell St • Glyndwr Rd

Quay Road • Bridge St • Mill Street • Park Avenue • P

South Marine Terrace • Rheidol Terr • Greenfield Terr • P

Trefechan Rd • Riverside Terr • P

WC

WC

WC

Norton Terrace

A44

Harbour

Jetty • Pen

history still stands on the sea front, and is considered by many to be the most interesting example of Victorian architecture in the town. It was built as a luxury hotel in 1860 by Thomas Savin, the railway pioneer, who sought to exploit Aberystwyth's potential as a popular seaside resort by offering a week's free holiday in the hotel to anyone buying a return ticket from London. But the project went bankrupt after devouring £80,000 and the building was snapped up for a mere £10,000 to become the first college of the future University of Wales. The well-known hymn Aberystwyth was composed here by Dr. Joseph Parry, and today the University College campus has aspired to a large modern site on Penglais Hill.

Aberystwyth is also home to the Welsh College of Agriculture and the College of Librarianship Wales. But the most impressive academic institution of all is the National Library of Wales - a building of classical styling and proportions, in a suitably elevated hillside location. The National Library is an Aladdin's cave of Welsh treasures - historical, cultural, literary and otherwise - as described on page 67.

Visitor attractions in Aberystwyth are many and varied. They include the excellent new marina and waterside facilities, the electric cliff railway and Vale of Rheidol narrow gauge steam railway - both reflecting the town's strong railway heritage - and the remarkable camera obscura perched on top of Constitution Hill. Pen Dinas headland, south of the town centre, is the site of a large Iron Age hillfort, while the Ceredigion Museum, housed in a delightfully-restored Edwardian music hall, evokes the spirit of much more recent history. Aberystwyth Arts Centre is also well patronised, as are the Castle Theatre and the Commodore Cinema.

As for Aberystwyth Castle, sadly very little remains. Building began in 1277, during the period when Edward I embarked on a massive programme of castle construction in the face of fierce Welsh revolt, mainly in the north. The huge fortresses at Flint, Conwy, Harlech and Caernarvon were all products of this strategy. The choice of site for Aberystwyth's castle, near the mouth of the Rheidol, was greatly influenced by the presence of a harbour, which provided a vital communications link and also enabled materials and labour to be brought in by sea. From 1404 to 1408 the castle was held by Owain Glyndwr, and more than two centuries later it was destroyed by Cromwell's forces in the Civil War. Shortly before this, however, Charles I had established a mint here, using silver from local mines, and some of the coins minted can be seen in the Ceredigion Museum.

Aberystwyth Arts Centre   Situated on Penglais Hill next to the National Library of Wales, with spectacular views over Cardigan Bay, Wales's largest and most exciting Arts Centre boasts a 900-seat concert hall and

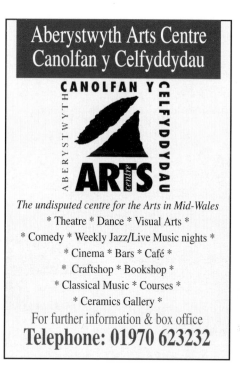

Aberystwyth Arts Centre
Canolfan y Celfyddydau

The undisputed centre for the Arts in Mid-Wales
* Theatre * Dance * Visual Arts *
* Comedy * Weekly Jazz/Live Music nights *
* Cinema * Bars * Café *
* Craftshop * Bookshop *
* Classical Music * Courses *
* Ceramics Gallery *
For further information & box office
Telephone: 01970 623232

View from Constitution Hill

300-seat theatre. It is one of the main venues in Wales for the performing and visual arts. The quality and scope of the Centre's programme is very impressive and attracts many top-name performers. Drama, light entertainment, music, dance, pantomime and a summer show are all part of the busy annual schedule. The Centre also has nationally-acclaimed gallery areas, a ceramics collection, craft shop, cafe and the Penglais Bookshop. For performance details and bookings, ring the box office on 01970 623232/622889.

Aberystwyth Marina (Y Lanfa) This outstanding new development has transformed Aberystwyth's old silted-up harbour and its immediate area into a major boating, recreational, shopping and residential centre of superlative quality. The waterside complex comprises shops, cafes, restaurant, pub, offices and luxury apartments. Boating facilities are first-class, with floating pontoons to accommodate 100 vessels and services that include electricity, water, a floating diesel fuel pump, a unique sewage pump-out system and holding tank, and security gates to prevent unlawful access to the pontoons. There are also secure boat parks, and visiting boats are welcome. For more information ring 01970 615800.

Aberystwyth Yesterday This exhibition is to be found in the first-floor hall above Aberystwyth railway station. It contains a large collection of photographs tracing the development of the town over a 150-year period. There are also displays of furniture and clothing, such as Victorian christening gowns and faithfully-reproduced nursery scenes. For more information ring 01970 617119.

Ceredigion Museum The Ceredigion

Museum has a fine collection of folk material housed in the Coliseum, a beautiful Edwardian theatre built in 1905 and later used as a cinema. The theatre was lovingly restored in 1983 to recapture its original inspiring ambience. The permanent displays illustrate the three main occupations which historically have earned the people of Ceredigion their living, namely agriculture, seafaring and lead mining. There are also displays on carpentry, spinning and weaving, clocks and furniture, domestic items and pottery, costume and military uniforms, along with a reconstruction of a traditional cottage. The new Bowen Gallery houses a comprehensive exhibition on the geology and archaeology of the area. Temporary exhibitions, displaying the work of local artists, are changed monthly. The entrance to the museum is via the Tourist Information Centre in Terrace Road, and admission is free. Facilities include a shop selling books and postcards, free worksheets for children, toilets and a lift for disabled visitors. The museum is open from 10.00am-5.00pm, Monday to Saturday, and on Sundays during school holidays. For more information ring 01970 633085.

Electric Cliff Railway One of two great Victorian attractions on Constitution Hill, this is the only cliff railway in Wales and the longest in Britain. The design of its 778-feet track and 6-compartment carriages is unique - the work of Croyden Marks, who also constructed the cliff railways at Lynton, Clifton and Bridgnorth. When it opened in 1896 it was water operated, but now a powerful electric motor drives the high-tensile steel ropes which haul the carriages up to the 430-ft summit. The railway makes 20,000 journeys a year, and its safety devices are impressive by any standards. For example, the steel ropes can take a load

CEREDIGION MUSEUM

TERRACE ROAD, ABERYSTWYTH
TEL: (01970) 633088

Monday - Saturday
10am-5pm
Open on Sundays during school holidays

ADMISSION FREE

Free Children's Quiz-Something for Everyone
"Probably the most beautiful museum interior in Britain"

greater than 10 times the weight of a fully-loaded carriage. There are 4 independent braking systems, capable of stopping a fully-loaded carriage within 9 inches. And the electronic controls are so accurate that the speed never varies from 4 mph, journey times by more than 1 second and carriage docking positions by more than 1 inch! For more information ring 01970 617642.

Great Aberystwyth Camera Obscura This re-creation of a popular Victorian amusement opened in 1985, and is the biggest camera obscura in the world. Its huge 14-inch lens takes in a bird's eye view of more than 1000 square miles of land and seascape in a 360° sweep around Aberystwyth, which is reflected on to a circular table screen in the darkened viewing gallery below. It is possible to see as many as 26 Welsh mountain peaks, including Snowdon. Admission to the Great Camera Obscura is free. It occupies a two-storey octagonal tower on top of Constitution Hill, and can be reached by footpath or the electric cliff railway. Light refreshments are available. For more information ring 01970 617642.

Llanbadarn Church Llanbadarn was originally a village in its own right but, located just a mile from the centre of Aberystwyth, it has gradually become a suburb of the town. The impressive 12th-century church is one of the biggest in Wales and contains a number of inscribed stones. St. Padarn founded a religious settlement here in the 6th century, and his life and work is depicted in a stained glass window. There is also a fascinating exhibition which features an early chapel, a cell where St. Padarn might have lived and a 13th Century Celtic church.

National Library of Wales See feature on page 67.

Penglais Nature Park Open all year round, this 27-acre park offers attractive woodland walks and the chance to see some of the area's rich variety of wildlife. In addition to the woods, which have a fine showing of bluebells in the spring and once formed part of the 18th-century Penglais Estate, the park features a quarry - the site for the Aberystwyth Panorama Viewpoint, from where the views over the town and Cardigan Bay are truly spectacular. For more information, ask for the Penglais Nature Park leaflet at any Tourist Information Centre.or ring the park on 01545 572142

Vale of Rheidol Railway Opened in 1902 to serve the lead mines, timber and passenger traffic of the Rheidol valley, this wonderful narrow gauge steam railway runs out of Aberystwyth station to Devil's Bridge, a distance of almost 12 miles. The line climbs over 600 feet and takes a leisurely 1 hour for the single journey - 3 hours return. For more information ring 01970 625819.

Borth & Ynyslas
Borth is a quiet but well-patronised resort, six miles north of Aberystwyth, whose long-lasting popularity was assured with the arrival of the Aberystwyth and Welsh Coast

Borth

Mammals, Birds, Reptiles and Invertebrates

 **B RTH**

Open daily from Easter till end of October

ANIMALARIUM

1/2 mile off Borth High Street

Come and see our collection of animals.

Enjoy a wide range of animals from creepy crawlies to the world's largest rodent. You may like to look at the familiar goats and rabbits. In the paddocks you will see wallabies and rare breeds of sheep. Admire the wonderful colours of the pheasants or watch the monkeys in the monkey house and mice in the mouse town and much more.

Telephone: 01970 871224

Railway in 1863. Borth's unique character and appeal is due to the fact that it stands on a spit of shingle; in front of its main street are four miles of sandy beach and the sea of Cardigan Bay, and behind it the impressive expanse of marshy peat bogland known as Cors Fochno. While the immediate landscape is uncharacteristically flat for West Wales, the scenery beyond is magnificent, with the Dovey estuary and southern extremities of Snowdonia to the north and the foothills of the Cambrian Mountains encircling the area to the east.

In winter Borth is at the mercy of the sea, and to protect the shingle ridge from the ravages of storms it is held in place by many rows of wooden groynes positioned along the beach. Summer is a different matter altogether, when Borth offers a good choice of accommodation - hotels, a holiday centre, self-catering and caravan and camp sites - and is a very popular resort for bathing, boating, watersports and fishing. Borth and

OPEN 10AM TO 10PM
A La Carte Menu
Lunchtime Menu – 12 noon to 3pm
Home cooked food
Wedding Receptions and Parties catered for
HIGH STREET, BORTH, CEREDIGION
TELEPHONE (01970) 871 803

Ynyslas Golf Club's championship links course is the oldest 18-hole course in Wales.

The marshy bog of Cors Fochno, part of which is a National Nature Reserve, contains many rare plants and is a refuge for birds and wildlife. Under threat for many years because of attempts to drain it and reclaim the land for agricultural use, the bog has now been declared a wetland of international importance and is protected.

The area around Borth is excellent

walking country. As well as coastal footpaths to Clarach and Aberystwyth, you can take the path to the War Memorial on top of Craig Y Wylfa headland, where the views on a clear day are spectacular in all directions. Of particular note are the rocky outcrops rising from the bog of Cors Fochno on which are built the church of St. Matthew and the hamlet of Llancynfelyn.

Ynyslas, which lies near the southern lip of the mouth of the Dovey estuary, is something of a naturalists' paradise. The wide sandy foreshore and delicate sand dunes, with their rich plant and animal life, are part of the Dyfi (Dovey) National Nature Reserve. This is managed by the Countryside Council for Wales and there is an information centre here. Just to the north-east of Ynyslas, along the shore of the Dovey estuary, is the RSPB reserve of Ynys Hir, while on the landward side of Ynyslas stretches the raised peat bog.

Most of the sand dunes at Ynyslas have been formed during the last few centuries. Until 1824 the River Leri flowed directly into Cardigan Bay near Ynyslas, but in that year it was diverted into the estuary. The effect was to stabilise the area of dunes to the north and the Twyni Mawr rapidly grew in size. The dunes are still expanding. By contrast, Cors Fochno is much older, its origins going back about 4000 years.

The wide flat sands at Ynyslas, known as Traeth Maelgwyn, are named after a notorious 6th-century Welsh prince whose cunning won him sovereignty of the western kingdoms. It is said that a meeting of princes was arranged on the sands near Aberdovey to unite them in the fight against Angle and Saxon invaders. It was agreed that chairs would be placed on the shore and whoever remained seated the longest as the tide came in would be declared King of Wales. Crafty Maelgwyn used a chair made of waxed birds' wings, and he stayed afloat while the other princes were well and truly sunk. The

ceremony is still re-enacted on the sands every year as part of Borth's carnival week.

Through the centuries, several methods were devised to cross the estuary to Aberdovey from Ynyslas. This included one of Britain's oldest ferries, which was moored on the Aberdovey side. To summon it you had to ring the bell which hung from a post on the shore. Among the ferry's more famous passengers were Lord Rhys in 1156, the great local poet Dafydd ap Gwilym, and the princes of Wales, who in 1215 were summoned by Llywelyn the Great to the Great Council of Aberdovey. Eventually there were three ferry services operating - one for coaches and heavy traffic; another for horse riders, cattle and luggage; and a third (an express service) for foot passengers.

In the days when the estuary was shallower, drovers crossed the Dovey to Ynyslas by fording the river at low tide. It must have been quite a sight as large numbers of cattle, sheep, pigs and other animals were herded across the sands by drovers and their dogs, en route for the Midlands and other English markets. Stops along the way included Llanbadarn Fawr (near Aberystwyth) and Tregaron. To protect their hooves on the long trek, cattle were fitted with iron shoes; even geese were shod, by making them walk through tar and feathers! The drovers also needed to protect large sums of money as they returned home across the desolate landscape, and they were instrumental in setting up many small banks in Ceredigion, such as the Aberystwyth and Tregaron Bank.

Ynyslas today has plenty to interest the many visitors who return each summer. In addition to its natural estuarine beauty and wide expanses of sand and fascinating bird and nature reserves, there are nearby attractions such as the 19th-century metal smelting works at Eglwysfach and the old chapel at Tre'r Ddol, which houses the Museum of Religious Life in Wales. A little further afield are the sights and amenities of Aberystwyth and the spectacular beauty of the Rheidol Valley and Plynlimon Hills.

Borth Animalarium One of the top attractions of mid Wales with a Wales Tourist Board seal of approval, Borth Animalarium is committed to the captive breeding of endangered species, many of which are now part of a national breeding programme. This conservation work, vital to protect animals facing extinction, is carried out in close conjunction with a number of zoos and the Northern Zoological Society based at Chester Zoo. Visitors can see all the animals at close quarters - breeding colonies of lemurs, owls, monkeys, capybaras, wallabies, polecats, racoons, birds and many others. Then there are attractions such as the bat and reptile houses, the collection of exotic insects, and animals such as cavies, rabbits, gerbils, pet lambs, pigmy goats, chipmunk and chinchillas. Many exhibits are under cover and the Animalarium, which is close to the beach, also has a picnic area, play area an educational room, souvenir shop and cafe serving light refreshments. It is open daily from Easter till the end of September. For more information ring 01970 871224.

Brynllys Organic Farm Walks Spend a few very enjoyable hours on this 250-acre family farm near Borth, seeing how organic farming and nature conservation go hand in hand. Three walks have been devised to show you the variety of wildlife habitats here, which include a traditional hay meadow, ponds, new woodland and hedgerows. The longest walk is 3 miles, the shortest only 1 mile, and en route are spectacular panoramic views over Borth Bog and the Dovey estuary. The farm also has a prize-winning pedigree herd producing organic milk, which is used in the making of Rachel's Dairy products - cream, butter, cheese and yoghurt - all available from the farm shop. Family groups

Ynyslas

of up to 6 can visit the farm free (March 1st-Nov 30th) but larger groups need to book for a conducted tour. And remember that this is a working farm, so suitable clothing and footwear are recommended. For more information ring 01970 871489.

Dyfi Furnace The wild, spectacular country of the Dovey estuary is not the obvious place to find a blast furnace. This unusual visitor attraction, an 18th-century foundry for smelting iron ore, is now under the care of Cadw (Welsh Historic Monuments) and originally gave the village of Furnace its name. The bellows that pumped air into the charcoal-fired blast furnace were powered by the waterwheel, which was driven by the force of the River Einion plunging down a waterfall. The waterwheel can be seen working throughout the main holiday season.

Tre'r Ddol Folk Museum This chapel museum, devoted to the 1859 Methodist Revival which began in Tre'r Ddol, contains much of interest. Apart from the religious section, there are crafts, domestic and farm objects, and Welsh furniture - all collected by the late R.J. Thomas, a distinguished Welsh scholar. Tre'r Ddol is situated due east of Ynyslas, on the A487.

Ynyslas Nature Reserve The wide beach and sand dune systems at Ynyslas form part of the Dyfi (Dovey) National Nature Reserve.

HOMELY KITCHEN
Cafe Bar & Restaurant

A cosy **cafe/restaurant** with a friendly atmosphere, mostly Welsh speaking staff and **good home cooked food** for all the family
Usual Opening Hours
Monday to Saturday
9.00 am to 5.30 pm
Evening and Sunday Bookings
available in the Summer
please telephone

Pendre, Cardigan
Telephone: 01239 621863

The Eagle Inn
Free House & Restaurant
Open 7 days a week for
Bar Meals • *Sunday Lunch and Real Ale*

Jimmy, Angela and Family
Castle Street • *Cardigan*
Tel.: 01239 612046

CROESO   WELCOME

This is managed by the Countryside Council for Wales, and there is a wildlife information centre and shop (open Easter to mid-September) standing within the dunes. You can enjoy the great scenic beauty of the estuary here at any time of year, and during the holiday season there is the bonus of guided walks (Sundays only), on which you can find out more about the complex nature of the dunes and the area's fascinating wildlife. Ynyslas provides plenty of parking space, for which there is only a nominal charge. For more information ring 01970 871640.

Cardigan

Historic Cardigan, beautifully sited near the mouth of the River Teifi - hence the town's Welsh name of Aberteifi - is an important holiday centre, with some of Wales' most attractive coast and countryside right on the doorstep. Just across the estuary is Pembrokeshire, with its magnificent national park and 186-mile coast path; stretching east from Cardigan is the scenic Teifi Valley; and to the north is the spectacular Ceredigion coastline and its many beaches and resorts.

Cardigan received its first royal charter in 1199 from King John and is the former county town. Still a thriving market town, it serves the local farming communities and is also the main shopping centre for South Ceredigion. The Market Hall, built in 1859 and featuring impressive stone arches, holds a general market twice weekly and a livestock market once a week. The old character of the town is retained by its shops and narrow streets, and the visitor attractions include the Theatr Mwldan (housed in the same building as the Tourist Information Centre), an indoor leisure centre, a golf club at nearby Gwbert, and a large annual arts festival, Gwyl Fawr Aberteifi. Cardigan is also the home of the national shrine of the Roman Catholic Church in Wales.

Crossing the Teifi below the castle is the striking multi-arched stone bridge. There appears to be disagreement as to whether this is the original Norman bridge, strengthened and widened in later years, or whether it was constructed in the 17th or even 18th century. The history of Cardigan Castle raises less argument: the ruins that now remain date from 1240, and it must have been in an earlier castle that the very first National Eisteddfod - 'advertised' for a whole year beforehand throughout Wales, England and Scotland - was hosted by Rhys ap Gruffudd in 1176. The National Eisteddfod is now the major cultural event in the Welsh calendar, as well as being Europe's largest peripatetic cultural festival, and is held in August at a different venue each year. Inevitably, Cardigan Castle was destroyed by Cromwell; all that remains is now privately owned.

A much more recent aspect of Cardigan's colourful history was its role as one of Wales' most prominent ports. As many as 300 ships were registered here and shipbuilding thrived in the 19th century. The busy warehouses along the waterfront handled everything from exports of herring, corn, butter and slate to imports of limestone, salt, coal, timber for shipbuilding, and manufactured goods. Human cargo was carried too: emigrant ships sailed from Cardigan to New York in the USA and New Brunswick in Canada.

Cardigan

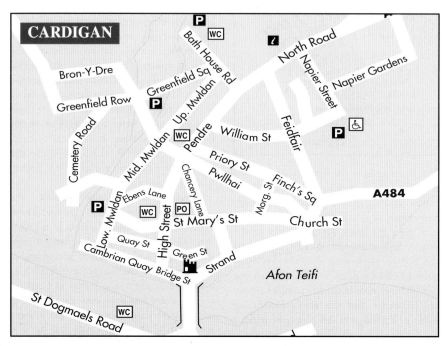

This prosperous period for Cardigan was relatively short-lived, however. Inevitably, booming trade meant that ships were getting bigger all the time while the gradual silting of the estuary was making access to Cardigan more and more restricted. The final nail in the port's coffin was the coming of the railway in 1885.

As a holiday centre, Cardigan has many attractions within easy reach. Across the river in Pembrokeshire stands St. Dogmael's Abbey and the popular beach of Poppit Sands, which marks the northern end of the 186-mile Pembrokeshire Coast Path. Along the Teifi, in a spectacular setting overlooking a deep wooded gorge, is Cilgerran Castle, which inspired a painting by Turner. In August, the annual coracle festival takes place along this stretch of the river.

Quixote Gift Shop, Cardigan If you're looking for a quality gift and you fancy a nostalgic trip down memory lane, Quixote is the place to visit. This leading gift shop will show you old-fashioned teddy bears - including Paddington and Pooh - and a whole range of ideas, from beautiful dried flower arrangements to exquisite jewellery in Victorian and Edwardian style. The shop is also one of the area's main stockists of Clogau Welsh gold jewellery, offering a wide selection of rings, earrings, brooches and necklaces. Other items on display include sheepskin rugs, festive candles and traditional Victorian Christmas decorations. This quaint little shop is located on Cardigan's College Row. For more information ring 01239 613119.

Cardigan Island This small island, less than 16 hectares in size, is the only one off the Ceredigion coast and is leased by Dyfed Wildlife Trust as a nature reserve, with no public access. It is situated at the mouth of the River Teifi. Every year the Trust conducts a census of the island's small colonies of seabirds. The lesser black-backed gulls are the dominant species, with only a few hundred herring gulls and very small numbers of other seabirds. In 1934, when the motor vessel Herefordshire was wrecked on the northern rocks, brown rats came ashore and annihilated the island's population of puffins. There have been various attempts to reinstate both puffins and Manx shearwaters; a few have bred but it is a long and slow process to establish healthy breeding colonies here again.

Cardigan Island Coastal Farm Park & Waterfowl Centre A cliff-top nature trail at Gwbert-on-Sea takes you to a headland within 200 yards of the island. The caves below the trail and around the island are breeding grounds for Atlantic grey seals, and bottle-nosed dolphins can also be seen here. The nature trail gives access to the farm's own animals and Waterfowl Centre. For

C. & M. MORRIS
Motor & Electrical Engineers
Crosslyn Garage, Blaenannerch, Cardigan
Tel: Aberporth (01239) 810386

M.O.T. Testing
Repair Service
Petrol & Shop

Retail Motor Industry Federation

MURCO

Quixote
"gift shoppe"
Come and browse in our 'Olde Worlde' shop. See our range of beautiful Welsh Clogau Gold, Memory Lane Collection of Cottages, table mats, leather goods and a large selection of candles. Also our lovely range of greetings cards, gift wrap and collectors postcards. Main stockist of the Bean Bag Tray, Spanish Green & Blue recycled glassware, Russ Soft Toys including adorable cuddly teddy-bears. Many more items for the whole family.

4 College Row, Cardigan
Tel: (01239) 613119

View towards Cardigan Island

more information ring 01239 612196.

Dyfed Shire Horse Farm, near Cardigan See page 69.

Felinwynt Rainforest & Butterfly Centre Step into this enlightening visitor attraction and you're immediately transported into a different world. The atmosphere of the rainforest is startlingly real as you wander through the tropical and native plants, listening to the recorded sounds of the unique Peruvian Amazon. Beautiful, exotic butterflies fly freely around you. The humidity needed to sustain the plants and butterflies is provided by the waterfall, ponds and stream, which are inhabited by fish and amphibians. There is no admission charge to the rainforest exhibition (based on the Tambopata Reserve in Peru). Posters, tee-shirts and other merchandise, sold in aid of rainforest projects, including Tambopata, can be found in the Centre's comprehensive gift shop. Light refreshments and cool drinks - butterflies are most active on sunny days - are also available. The Centre is 6 miles from Cardigan and 4 miles from Aberporth, on the Aberporth to Ferwig road, 2 miles from the A487 turn-off to Aberporth at Blaenannerch. Follow the signs to Felinwynt. For more information ring 01239 810882.

Gelli Aur Nursery, Bird Gardens & Arboretum Ornamental trees, rare shrubs, waterfowl, peacocks and pygmy goats can all be found here. The arboretum contains over 100 varieties of trees and incorporates a play area, picnic area and interesting walkways. As well as a nursery stocking thousands of quality plants, the landscape gardens include ponds and waterfalls. There are also exotic birds from all over the world including waterfowl and decorative pheasants. This 4-acre attraction is 7 miles from Cardigan, on the B4333 near Gogerddan crossroads. For more information ring 01239 811096.

St. Dogmael's Abbey See page 70.

Theatr Mwldan, Cardigan A 200-seat theatre and cinema located in historic buildings, Theatr Mwldan is one of Wales's leading arts and entertainment centres, host to a varied and lively programme of top-quality drama, light entertainment, music,

FELINWYNT RAINFOREST AND BUTTERFLY CENTRE

Enjoy a unique visit to the Tropical House where visitors can wander midst exotic plants and tropical butterflies. Relax in the tea room or browse in the shop, watch the video and study the rainforest exhibition.

Open every day from the beginning of May to the end of September
Admission charge only to the Tropical House

Follow the Rainforest Centre signs from Blaenannerch on the A487 6 miles north of Cardigan.

Tel:(01239) 810882

dance and film. For performance details and bookings, ring the box office on 01239 621200.

Cei Bach

It is hard to imagine that small and peaceful Cei Bach (which is Welsh for Little Quay) could ever have been a hive of industry. Yet Ceredigion's 19th-century surge in shipbuilding even reached the shores of this quiet bay. Furthermore, Cei Bach at one time had four limekilns in operation, serviced by limestone brought from South Wales on coastal trading vessels. The lime which the kilns produced was much in demand by farmers to combat the area's notoriously acidic clay soils and to aid drainage. Another use for this valuable resource was to mix lime with clay and coal dust to produce round balls known as pale - a slow-burning fuel that was ideal for the cottage fire. The remains of two of Cei Bach's four kilns can still be seen.

Near to Cei Bach is tiny Llanina Church, with its mystery of the church beneath the sea. It is said that Ina, 7th-century King of the West Saxons and builder of Glastonbury Abbey, was shipwrecked off the coast and rescued by local inhabitants. As a gesture of thanksgiving he built a church on an outcrop of rock known as Cerrig Ina (Ina's stones). But the church was swallowed up by the encroaching sea. The present-day Llanina Church was built in 1850.

Cilgerran

This small village on the Teifi hosts an annual coracle regatta in August and boasts two major visitor attractions:

Cilgerran Castle Cilgerran Castle is 3 miles south-east of Cardigan, in a dramatic position on a high bluff above the River Teifi. Seen from the deep wooded gorge below - as it was for centuries by the coracle fishermen - it presents a spectacular sight which inspired great landscape artists such as Turner and Richard Wilson. Equally, the views which visitors can enjoy from its

View from Cilgerran Castle

ruined towers are magnificent. The castle, small by comparison with Pembroke and the great Norman fortresses of North Wales, is mainly 13th century. Despite its apparently unassailable position, the castle changed hands many times between the 12th and 14th centuries. For further information ring 01239 615007

Welsh Wildlife Centre, Cilgerran Managed by Dyfed Wildlife Trust, this 265-acre nature reserve comprises an interesting variety of habitats - marsh, reedbed, woodland, mudflat and river bank. There is also an award winning visitor centre housing a fully accessible exhibition area. You will also find a children's playground, gift shop and a restaurant, with fine views over the marshes and river towards Cardigan.New for 1998 was the 'Water World' featuring water wildlife and other mini-beasts. For further information ring 01239 621600.

Clarach

The sandy bay of Clarach is a popular holiday centre, sheltered between two steep hills. One of these is the northern slope of Constitution Hill, over which a very scenic, mile-long nature trail takes you to

Clarach

Aberystwyth. Following the coast in the opposite direction brings you to Borth.

Clarach has extensive caravan and chalet developments. The bay lies at the mouth of the river of the same name, and the broad U shape of the Clarach Valley is a fine example of a valley cut by the unstoppable progress of a glacier during the last Ice Age. The steep shale cliffs which shelter the beach are at least 400 million years old and show distinct signs of folding and other distortion caused by the tremendous forces of earth movements. Caves show where the sea has eroded weaker points in the rocks, while harder outcrops stand as upright columns, or stacks, which are favourite perches for shags, cormorants and other seabirds.

A little way up the Clarach Valley is Llangorwen, which has an 18th-century stone bridge and a 19th-century church with a tall tower and spire.

Cwmtydu

Cwmtydu (also commonly spelt Cwmtudu) lies south-west of New Quay along a section of Heritage Coast. The beach of this secluded cove is popular in summer and there is a superb coastal walk across the National Trust headland.

A little further north along the coast, near the mouth of the River Soden, is the site of Castell Bach - an Iron Age promontory fort occupied by Celts from around the 3rd century BC. The camp consisted of two enclosures bounded by ditches and by earthen banks topped with timber fencing. The inner circle was the living area, with round thatched-roofed huts and raised storage structures, and the outer enclosure served as a stock compound. These early tribes lived mainly by their stock rearing, probably supplemented by fishing, growing crops and hunting for deer and wild boar. A few specialised crafts also developed. Spindle whorls and simple looms were used to make cloth from wool and flax which was coloured with natural dyes.

Devil's Bridge & the Rheidol Valley

In a very picturesque setting at the head of the Rheidol Valley, among the wooded hills of Plynlimon, Devil's Bridge is one of Wales' most famous and spectacular beauty spots. For here you will find the enchanting narrow-gauge steam railway, snaking its way through the valley to Aberystwyth twelve miles away, and the magnificent Mynach Falls. As for the bridge which gives the village its name, there are in fact three bridges - built one on top of the other.

Whether you take the train to Devil's Bridge or travel here by car, the scenery is stunning. The Plynlimon Hills, liberally decorated with forest and cascading streams, rise to almost 1000 feet above sea level and provide one of Britain's last retreats for the rare red kite. But to many visitors the most impressive sight has to be the falls themselves, created by the Mynach river as it tumbles more than 300 feet down the narrow gorge and spills into the River Rheidol below Devil's Bridge.

The Mynach Falls, for a long time part of the Hafod Estate, are still in private ownership and you have to pay a modest fee

Devil's Bridge

Devil's Bridge Station

to see them. Admission is through a turnstile, but you should take note that walking the paths down to the falls and back up again is fairly strenuous and could present major problems to the disabled or infirm. The last part of the descent is on the zigzagging Jacob's Ladder, which has nearly 100 steps taking you right to the bottom of the dark and hidden gorge, or the 'dread chasm' as it was christened by William Wordsworth in 1824. From here you can view the three bridges and the falls in all their splendour.

A separate and shorter walk, also via a turnstile, takes you to the Devil's Punchbowl (or Cauldron as it is also referred to) where the action of the cascading water has carved out huge cavities in the rock at the bottom of the falls. Here too you can see the remarkable sight of the three bridges stacked on top of each other.

The first of the bridges to be built was a simple medieval stone structure, and is known in Welsh as Pont-y-gwr Drwy (the Bridge of the Evil One). According to legend, the Devil came across a weeping old woman named Megan Llandunach whose cow was stuck on the other side of the gorge. He offered to provide a bridge, on condition that he could claim the first living thing to cross it. But the old woman outwitted him by throwing a crust across the bridge for a hungry dog to chase. In reality it is likely that the bridge was built by either the Knights Templars or the monks of Strata Florida Abbey, in the latter case to reach the sheep pastures on the other side. What is certain is that the bridge had been built by 1188, since Gerald of Wales states in his writings that he crossed the bridge in that year.

There is some uncertainty as to the date of the second bridge; some sources quote 1708, others say 1753. It was built directly above the first and is also made of stone, though it has a much bigger span and is wider, presumably to take horse-drawn vehicles. The decorative cast-iron balustrade was added in 1814, along with other improvements.

Atop these two bridges is the present road bridge, an iron structure with a 60-foot span. It was built in 1901 and modernised in 1983.

Another notable landmark near the falls is the Hafod Arms Hotel, constructed in the 1830's in the style of a large Swiss chalet by the fourth Duke of Newcastle. The hotel terrace enjoys tremendous views across the gorges.

The area around Devil's Bridge was supposedly the haunt of a 16th-century gang of robbers and murderers. Three of the gang lived in a cave below the gorge and were called the bat children. But the law caught up with them and they were smoked out of their grim hideout and subsequently hanged at Rhayader. A trip to Devil's Bridge and the surrounding hills and countryside should be on the schedule of every visitor to Ceredigion. There are many fascinating things to see here, including the remains of a

prehistoric stone circle in the churchyard at Ysbyty Cynfyn. Other attractions, including the Llywernog Silver-Lead Mine and the Forestry Commission's Bwlch Nant-yr-Arian Visitor Centre, are described in the entry under Ponterwyd on page 53.

Hafod Trail This 2-mile walk takes you through picturesque river and mountain scenery of the Ystwyth Valley a few miles south of Devil's Bridge, between Cwmystwyth and Pontrhydygroes. It follows many of the paths created two centuries ago by Thomas Johnes for visitors to the Pleasure Grounds of Hafod Mansion. Johnes, an MP, landscaped the grounds between 1783 and 1815 in a style known as the Picturesque. His twin objectives were to complement the natural beauty of the Yswyth Valley and to encourage visitors to appreciate the variety and irregularity of nature through its constantly-changing scenes. In a period of 17 years he planted 5-6 million trees, most of which were raised in the Hafod nursery.

A long-term programme of partial restoration of the gardens, paths and landscape features at Hafod was started by the Forestry Commission in 1987 and is still under way. The work has included the complete restoration in 1988 of the Bedford Monument - a neo-classical obelisk erected by Johnes in 1805 to commemorate the 5th Duke of Bedford, who died in 1802.

A booklet describing the Hafod Trail is available from the Forestry Commission.

Rheidol Hydro-Electric Power Station The Information Centre combines an audio-visual exhibition and video show with a souvenir shop and refreshments. You can tour the power station and fish farm. At night the Felin Newydd Weir is spectacularly floodlit. For more information ring 01970 880670.

Vale of Rheidol Railway See page 27

WE PUT SOMETHING

Enjoy a day out in the beautiful and secluded Rheidol Valley, just ten miles from

BACK INTO THE

Aberystwyth. With its scenic drive, nature trails, excellent fishing opportunities and

ENVIRONMENT

the educational value provided by the Visitors Centre and tours of the power station

- YOU AND

at the Rheidol Hydro-Electric Scheme, this really is the ideal family excursion.

YOUR FAMILY

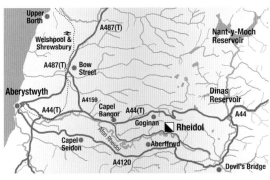

Visitors Centre
Free Entry. Open 1030 - 1615
1st April - 31st October

Station Tours
1100 - 1530
Free guided tours are available
daily, throughout the season.
No booking necessary.
Group tours are available all year
round by prior appointment.

Fishing
For disabled anglers, easy access
is provided at Dinas Lake.

Cwm Rheidol Dam
Lit from dusk till
2300 (BST), 2200 (GMT).

POWERGEN

FOR NOW AND FUTURE GENERATIONS

For more information contact: Rheidol Power Station, Cwm Rheidol, Aberystwyth, Ceredigion SY23 3NF, UK.
Tel: +44 (0) 1970 880667. Fax: +44 (0) 1970 880670. Photograph shows Cwm Rheidol Reservoir, Aberystwyth.

Gwbert

Gwbert-on-Sea is a small, quiet hamlet on the eastern shore of the mouth of the Teifi estuary, just a couple of miles outside Cardigan. The settlement takes its name from a wandering saint; St. Gwbert is said to have landed here and sheltered in a cave. The shoreline is marked by rugged cliffs and small shingle bays, with large stretches of sand bank exposed at low tide, and the area gives superb views over a diverse and scenic landscape: the ancient oak woodland of the Teifi Valley, the tidal marshes of the estuary, and the boundary of the Pembrokeshire Coast National Park. The 18-hole golf course - the home of Cardigan Golf Club - also offers fine views of the estuary and sea, and from the headland you can look across to Cardigan Island.

The mud and sand flats of the estuary attract a great variety of birds. In the autumn such waders as the redshank, oystercatcher and curlew can be seen feeding here, along with several species of migratory duck. Terns, cormorants, mute swans and herons are also regular visitors.

The headland of Craig y Gwbert is the site of an Iron Age fort. Pieces of pottery and fragments of leather footwear, believed to date from the 13th century, have also been found near Gwbert, and are now on display in Cardigan Museum.

Lampeter

Lampeter lies in pleasant pastoral countryside in the upper Teifi Valley, separated from Carmarthenshire by the river itself. This peaceful rural setting belies the fact that all roads seem to lead here: not only from Aberystwyth, Tregaron, Aberaeron and Cardigan, but also from towns south of the Teifi such as Carmarthen, Llandovery and Newcastle Emlyn. The reason is that Lampeter is not only a bustling market town, but an eminent seat of learning and the oldest university town in Wales.

St. David's University College was founded here in 1822 by Thomas Burgess, Bishop of St. David's. It was his wish that Welsh students who could not afford to attend Oxford or Cambridge could come here for a university education. The Harford family shared his vision and generously donated money and the Castle Field as the site for the new college. This duly opened in 1827 and was modelled on the neo-Gothic style of the Oxbridge colleges. One of its more famous early pupils was Charles Scott, son of Sir Walter Scott, and the library houses a large collection of medieval manuscripts and first editions. In 1965 the college was greatly expanded as part of the University of Wales, with new halls of residence and the admission of female students for the first time.

In complete contrast to the studious atmosphere of the university halls, market days in Lampeter are noisy, colourful affairs, attracting crowds of people from the many surrounding farmlands. Lampeter and the neighbouring town of Tregaron take it in turns to host the large weekly agricultural livestock market, Lampeter on alternate

Lampeter

Mondays and Tregaron on alternate Tuesdays, and each town holds a general market on alternate Tuesdays. (These arrangements are subject to change and you can check by ringing the Tourist Information Centre in Tregaron on 01974 298144.)

Lampeter also has a number of small shops which reflect the traditional trades and crafts of the Teifi Valley. For example, there are men's and women's outfitters, craft shops and furnishing outlets, and the town's wide main street is a pleasant mix of Victorian and Georgian architecture.

The coaching inns are a throwback to the 18th century, when drovers gathered at Lampeter before setting off across the hills with cattle and sheep to various markets in England. No doubt many were tempted by the offer of cheap brandy and tobacco, brought in by smugglers from France and Ireland and sold illegally at well below market price in Lampeter and Tregaron.

Earlier in Lampeter's history, the Normans had recognised that the town was a strategically important crossing point of the Teifi and they built a castle to protect it. All that remains of the castle is a large earth mound in the grounds of the college. Little is known about the castle, though records suggest it was attacked by Owain Gwynedd in the 12th century and put under siege by Owain Glyndwr in the 15th century. It is also thought that an earlier castle might once have stood to the north of Lampeter's parish church.

As a holiday centre, Lampeter has a lot to offer. The countryside all around provides excellent walks and superb views of the picturesque Teifi Valley, which attracts many anglers by virtue of its salmon, trout and sea trout. Golfers are well catered for at nearby Cilgwyn, and other attractions in the area include Castell Howell Leisure Park, Theatr Felin Fach, Brooklands Model Aircraft Museum, Siwan Woollen Mill, the National Coracle Centre, the Welsh Gold Centre in Tregaron, and the Dolaucothi Gold Mines.

A few miles south-west of Lampeter, on the Carmarthenshire side of the River Teifi, is Llanybydder. This is another of West Wales' small market towns which enjoys an international reputation, since its monthly horse sales are very well known and the high quality of the stock attracts buyers from all over the world.

Dolaucothi Roman Gold Mines One of only three gold mines in the entire Roman empire, the 2000-year-old Dolaucothi mine is today owned by the National Trust. For more information ring 01558 650359.

Felin yr Aber Water Mill This traditional Cardiganshire water-powered corn mill. is situated on a small farm, and there is abundant wildlife around the mill pond and the rivers Teifi and Grannell. It stands near Llanwnnen, south west of Lampeter. For more information ring 01570 480956.

Model Aircraft Exhibition The Model Aircraft Museum is near Cellan, 2 miles east of Lampeter on the B4343. It houses 500 models of aircraft which have served with the Fleet Air Arm and Royal Air Force from 1920 to the present day. Conducted tours outline the history of the RAF, and scenes from the Battle of Britain are realistically depicted using large dioramas, sound effects and

Black Lion Royal Hotel
HIGH STREET, LAMPETER, CEREDIGION SA48 7BG

Owners Edyfed, Janet & children Emlyn & Rowena Jones

The Black Lion Royal Hotel is an old coaching inn dating back to the 16th century. The hotel has a lot of character and natural charm. All bedrooms are en suite with satellite TV, direct dial phones, tea & coffee facilities. The Stable Bar and The Residents Bar both offer excellent menus with a good selection of vegetarian dishes, a grill menu or the exquisite Table d'Hotel menu. The hotel once again has its own stretch of private fishing on the River Teify and its own pheasant shoot. Situated in the University market town of Lampeter where a good selection of ladies and gents designer label fashion shops may be found.

TEL: 01570 422172

CROESO CYNNES I BAWB.
A warm welcome is extended to every one.

commentary. The museum supports a worthy cause, as all proceeds are given to the RAF Benevolent Fund. For details of opening times and conducted tours, ring 01570 422604.

Noah's Ark This working smallholding near Lampeter is a centre for rare breeds of farm animals and poultry. These include fancy fowl, ducks, geese and many others. For more information ring 01570 470333.

Llanbadarn Fawr

This ancient and influential religious settlement, formerly a village, is now a suburb of Aberystwyth. Its surprisingly large 13th-century church stands on the site of a 6th-century Celtic monastery founded by St. Padarn, and is considered to be one of the most interesting churches in Wales. Among its treasures are two impressive Celtic crosses. Both date from the 10th century and one of them is elaborately carved. The church, which has distinctive square towers, also boasts fine acoustics. For more information see page 27.

Llanbadarn Fawr is just one mile east of Aberystwyth town, and is also remembered as the birthplace of Dafydd ap Gwilym, whose reputation as the greatest of the medieval Welsh poets earned him European stature. Today the old village is overlooked by the joint campus of the College of Librarianship Wales, the Welsh Agricultural College and the College of Further Education.

Llandysul

More than any other town in the Teifi Valley, Llandysul has depended on the river for its living. When the valley's Welsh woollen mills were at their most prosperous, in the latter part of the last century and the early years of this, Llandysul was the busiest weaving centre in Wales. Water from the river was in plentiful supply, both to scour and wash the raw wool and fabrics and to turn the wheels of the woollen mills. Rock Mill at Capel Dewi - one of several working mills which survive in the area - still uses water power to drive some of its machinery. The wheel also generates electricity for the mill, and at one time even supplied power to the local church!

Today, the river is important to Llandysul for another industry: tourism. Anglers are attracted here by salmon and sea trout, and white-water canoeing through foaming rapids is a very popular activity.

Llandysul is also a pleasant market town, and well known as the home of Gomer Press, one of Wales' most important publishers. Notable features of the town include the restored 13th-century Norman church of St. Tysul's, with its square tower and grand painted arches. Inside the church is a stone which bears a 6th-century inscription.

Not surprisingly, the surviving woollen and flour mills are also a major draw to visitors. The Museum of the Welsh Woollen Industry stands a few miles west of Llandysul at Drefach Felindre. Working mills such as Curlew Weavers are only too pleased to show visitors their tweeds, flannels and Welsh tapestries. Material can be bought by the yard, or made up into any of a wide range of products - from baby blankets to bed spreads, table mats to travel rugs.

In the hills around Llandysul are numerous Iron Age forts such as Carn Wen, which has a high wall composed entirely of loose rock. Although the inhabitants of these forts were prehistoric, they would probably have shaken their heads in disbelief at seeing a game of cnapan in progress. Cnapan was a traditional but violent game played between the men of Llandysul and Llanwenog - two towns 8 miles apart - the object being to knock the ball against the opposing side's church door. Each game must have claimed many casualties, and in 1833 both towns were finally persuaded to give it up in favour of more civilised contests!

Castell Howell Leisure & Activity Centre

Castell Howell is set in 85 acres of rolling countryside, providing breathtaking views throughout the changing seasons. Peace and relaxation come naturally in this environment, but for those who want a more exhilarating stay, they can take part in a wide range of indoor and outdoor activities which suit all age groups.

The purpose built Leisure Centre and spacious lawns ensure that children can play safely. At the back of the cottages are fields and trees, and miles of glorious countryside. Adjacent to the Leisure Centre we have a Deer park enclosure, which this year is home to 6 hinds and their 4 calves born in June 1997. This year we have the added attraction of grass Go-Karting for you to experience.

Clay pigeon shoots are regularly organised at the top of the valley. We run our own gun club and can cater for both the novices to shooting and the experienced shot. Instruction is available if required. We have our own Riding stables and also can arrange riding lessons with our fully qualified instructor. The Leisure Centre has a heated indoor swimming pool with a small splashpool at the side, a sauna, squash courts and a games room with table tennis, pool tables and various games machines. The Castle Bar has a full children's license and serves good value bar meals. In the summer we often have barbecues.

Also at the top of the valley you will discover a small lake, stocked with rainbow trout - the perfect spot for a picnic or perhaps some relaxing fly-fishing. If you like walking, you will find in the valley an abundance of wildlife to observe. Less than a mile away we have a family of rare Red Kites who regularly fly overhead.

Entrance and parking is Free – just pay for the facilities that you use.
We are on the B4459 midway between Talgarreg and Pontsian.
Telephone : 01545 590209 for opening hours and information.
Open ALL year.

River Teifi

Castell Howell Holiday Centre The Centre's all-weather entertainment caters for every age and interest. For more information ring 01545 590209.

Curlew Weavers This well-known, family-run mill produces a wide range of woollen fabrics and products, including tweeds, flannels and curtain and upholstery materials. The shop, open all year round, has everything from bargain-price knitting wools to casual tops, skirts, dresses, coats, blankets and bedspreads. To find Curlew Weavers you will need to follow these directions carefully:

approaching from the south on the A487, take the B4333 and turn first left and second right; approaching from the north on the A487, take the B4334 for 1.8 miles and turn right, then first right again, first left and first left; from Newcastle Emlyn take the B4571 for 3.7 miles and turn left, first right and first left. For more information ring 01239 851357.

Rock Mills - Y Felin Wlan The mill is a Grade 2 listed building and was built in 1890 by John Morgan, the great-grandfather of the present proprietor. The River Clettwr, a

Curlew Weavers

FREE ADMISSION
CURLEW WEAVERS
WOOLLEN MILL
Rhydlewis. Tel 01239 851357

Produce a wide range of woollen fabrics, travel rugs, throws, bedspreads, shawls, ties, curtains, upholstery and garments. Mill & Shop open all year Mon–Fri 9am–5pm. Closed Bank Holidays. By appointment at other times. Situated midway between Llangrannog & Newcastle Emlyn.

Take B4333 or B4334 off A487 and follow our signs.
From Newcastle Emlyn take B4571 for 3.7 miles then follow our signs.

tributary of the Teifi, still drives what is a rare example of a double-width overshoot waterwheel. The mill produces bedspreads, blankets, rugs and other items from pure new wool, and sells a wide range of woollen products, crafts and gifts in the shop. It is located just east of Llandysul at Capel Dewi, on the B4459, which joins both the A475 and A485. For more information ring 01559 362356.

Llangrannog

A small but popular resort six miles south-west of New Quay, Llangrannog is in a unique position amid some of the most dramatic cliff scenery of Ceredigion's Heritage Coast. The village is squeezed into a deep and wooded narrow valley, at the foot of which is a fine sandy cove sheltered by towering cliffs. It is a very picturesque setting, and the walks and views along the cliff tops are spectacular.

Originally a religious settlement which survived on farming and fishing, Llangrannog developed as a port in the late 18th century and the sheltered creek became a haven for coastal trading vessels. It's hard to imagine it today, but shipbuilding and other industries flourished here. One of the main imports was limestone, and an unused limekiln still stands on the southern side of the village.

Much easier to picture is how the secluded coves and steep cliffs around Llangrannog provided perfect cover for smuggling - another thriving coastal activity in the 18th century. For example, just to the north of Llangrannog is the fine sandy beach of Cilborth, tucked away in a hidden cove and at low tide easily accessible along the foreshore.

You can also reach Cilborth from the Heritage Coast footpath, the start of which is marked by steps which have been cut into the cliff above Llangrannog beach. The views from this path are magnificent as it runs

north across the cliffs and skirts the prehistoric hillfort of Pendinaslochdyn. From here the long narrow peninsula of Ynys-Lochtyn, owned by the National Trust, thrusts out into Cardigan Bay in spectacular fashion, and must be one of the best viewpoints along the entire West Wales coast. Standing up here on a windy day is breathtaking in every sense; it can also be dangerous in such conditions, and great care should be taken.

Walking on along the coast beyond Ynys-Lochtyn brings you to Ceredigion's highest cliff - Penmoelciliau, standing 709 feet above the pounding seas. Needless to say, the views here are also something to write home about.

Llangrannog is the ideal base for those who like to combine days on the beach with long walks along the cliffs. The Welsh League of Youth (Urdd Gobaith Cymru) has a holiday centre here.

Countryside Collection at the Penbontbren Farm Hotel, is this unusual collection-cum-museum of old farm implements. For more information ring 01239 810248.

Cwmrhydneuadd Golfing and Fishing The interesting 9-hole golf course presents a challenge even to experienced players, but no handicap certificate is required and all are welcome. Complementing the golf are well-stocked lakes - a real temptation for fly fishermen. For more information ring 01239 654933.

Llangrannog Ski Centre See page 62.

Llanrhystud

Located 7 miles south-west of Aberystwyth on the main A487 coast road, Llanrhystud is a village of attractive 19th-century houses running alongside the little River Wyre. Agriculture is important here, as the village nestles on the edge of the fertile

Llangrannog

coastal plain and is separated from the sea by meadowland. There are two beaches within a mile of Llanrhystud (as described on page 10), where the river flows into Cardigan Bay, and the cliffs extending north to Monk's Cave are a designated section of Heritage Coast.

The area around Llanryhstud is of great historical interest. There are traces of several ancient settlements here, such as the two rounded mounds south of the village. One is Castell Mawr (the great castle) and the other is Castell Bach (the small castle), both of which were Iron Age hillforts. Between the two is a gully with the rather chilling name of 'the dell of slaughter' - reference to an ancient battle. To the east of the village, and overlooking it, you can see the remains of a ring and bailey castle on Caer Penrhos. The castle was built in 1148 by Cadwaladr Ap Gruffydd, a prince of North Wales, and fifty years later it was burned to the ground to prevent it falling into enemy hands. Two hundred years before this, in 988, Llanrhystud itself had been the target of invading forces when the village was destroyed by Vikings.

Llanrhystud church was rebuilt last century. The original tower was buttressed and topped with a broach spire. This is an unusual feature in this part of Wales, and a very distinctive landmark.

Llansantffraid & Llanon

These two small villages, just over three miles north of Aberaeron, are practically joined together. The main A487 coast road to Aberystwyth runs through Llanon, while on the low coastal apron to the seaward side is the older hamlet of Llansantffraid.

The villages are most unusual in that both have churches with dedications to female saints. Llanon takes its name from St. Non, the mother of St. David, who according to legend was born here around 500 AD. His birth is commemorated by the Non Stone in Aberystwyth Museum. The church in Llanon has a depression in one of its walls - reputedly made by a shot fired from a parliamentary warship in the Civil War.

St. Ffraid (St. Bridget), whose church gives Llansantffraid its name, was the patron saint of dairy maids and the daughter of an Irish chief. She founded the famous monastery at Kildare, where she died in 523 AD. The slate-clad parish church dates from the 7th century and has a 13th-century tower and an 18th-century interior, with gallery, box-pews, clear window glass, and brass chandeliers.

The two villages, lying between the rivers Peris and Cledan, developed from these small Celtic communities to occupy the area known as Morfa Esgob (Bishop's Meadows). This 100-acre area is of interest to historians, as it is an excellent and rare example of a medieval system of farming whereby land was divided into strips, or slangs. Each slang was separated from the next by furrows, stones or hedges, producing a patchwork quilt effect on the landscape. The slangs were rented to individuals for agricultural use - presumably in much the same way as modern-day allotments - and they shared common grazing rights in winter. This single-field system is unchanged for centuries, and some of the slangs are still used for grazing and growing crops.

The villages also enjoy a long tradition of seafaring, and many boats were built at the Peris Yard in the 19th century. Fishing was another ancient occupation, and the remains of fish traps which were supposedly constructed by the monks of Strata Florida Abbey are visible at the mouth of the River Cledan.

Mwnt

Beautiful, unspoilt and isolated, yet easily accessible, Mwnt is in the care of the National Trust and is a sheer delight for anyone looking for an alternative to the more

Mwnt

populated resorts of Cardigan Bay. Mwnt's charm is that it offers three attractions - namely a fine sheltered beach lying below the cliffs; a 250-ft hill which gives magnificent coastal views, and from which the place takes its name (Mwnt in Welsh is Traeth y Mwnt - the Beach of the Mound); and the tiny medieval Church of the Holy Cross, which dates from around 1400 and occupies an earlier Celtic site.

So on reaching Mwnt you have the choice of going up the steep path to the top of the mount, where the panoramic views are worth the effort, or down the zigzagging steps to the beach. These steps take you past an old limekiln - a reminder of the days when limestone was landed here and manhandled up the slope to avoid the extortionate tolls imposed on the turnpike roads.

The superb beach is a small sandy cove which faces west and is protected from winds by the headland. So it is a natural sun trap and idyllic in summer. Less appealing,

though, is the idea that in 1155 a battle was fought here between the Welsh and the Flemings. The home forces successfully repelled the invaders - a victory which, until the turn of the 19th century, was celebrated with an annual mock battle held on the first Sunday in January, known as Sul Coch (Bloody Sunday).

The isolated position of the whitewashed medieval Holy Cross Church (Eglwys y Graig) means that it was obscured from the view of passing seaborne raiders, for whom churches and their treasures were rich targets. It is probable that pilgrims landed at Mwnt in the 6th and 7th centuries on their way to Bardsey Island, the traditional burial ground of the Celtic saints.

New Quay

Clinging to a steep wooded hillside with views along the coast towards Aberaeron and Aberystwyth, New Quay is a picturesque and popular resort where life in summer revolves around the harbour and award-winning beaches. Sailing, fishing and watersports are among the main attractions - not surprisingly for a village which at one time was a prosperous fishing port and shipbuilding centre, but which today is one of the favourite beauty spots on the West Wales tourist map. There is certainly a broad choice of accommodation in New Quay and neighbouring Little Quay Bay, including camping and caravan sites, small hotels, and guest houses.

Relaxation is high on the agenda too. You can sit on the promenade and overlook the yachts and pleasure craft in the sheltered

New Quay

CAMBRIAN HOTEL

New Road, New Quay, Cardiganshire SA45 9SE
Telephone (01545) 560295

A fully licensed small family hotel under the personal supervision of the owners Terry and Maureen Annette. Situated in a quiet position on the outskirts of the town, with splendid views of the harbour and

Cardigan Bay. All our rooms are 'En-suite' with full central heating, colour TV, razor points, hair driers, trouser press, radio alarms and tea/coffee making facilities. There is ample car parking, gardens and patio. There are several safe beaches within walking distance. The restaurant which is open to non residents has a full 'A la carte' menu and a happy family atmosphere.

NEW QUAY HONEY FARM

VISIT THE LARGEST BEE CENTRE IN WALES

◆ EXHIBITION OF LIVE BEES AND ANTS ◆
◆ HONEY SHOP ◆ MEADERY ◆ TEA ROOM ◆
PICNIC AREA ◆ FREE PARKING ◆

A working honey farm, with an exhibition, where the fascinating world of the honey bee can be observed behind glass in complete safety. A hive that opens up so that you can see right into the heart of the colony, audio visual displays and an ant colony completes the exhibition.

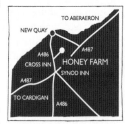

1/2 mile off the Synod Inn to Newquay Road.

Set in an old chapel on a beautiful farm near New Quay, this popular visitor attraction was established 6 years ago by Mariana and Gerald Cooper. This year the attraction has been further extended with a new meadery and small exhibition, which shows the history of mead and how it is made, an ant colony, which shows how other social insects co-operate, and new products in the shop. The exhibition shows live bees in a variety of habitats, and, along with the audio visual display enables the visitor to gain an insight into the importance of the bees' role in the natural world. The tearoom sells cream teas, homemade cakes and light meals, and in the honey shop you will find everything from honey, honey marmalade, honey beer, mead and other honey products made on the farm, to beeswax candles, cosmetics, polish, beekeeping equipment, books and quality local crafts.

There are two other good reasons for visiting New Quay Honey farm. One is the beneficial properties of honey. The other is that honey produced in this area is of very high quality, due to the abundance of wild flowers and trees that flourish in this unspoilt corner of Wales. The honey is extracted with the maximum of care and attention, and is not pasteurised. In this way it comes to you in the best possible condition. The farm is open from Easter to November 1st 7 days a week from 10 to 6. The exhibition is open every day from May 1st to November 1st. The shop is also open throughout the winter from 11 to 4 on Fridays, Saturdays and Sundays. For more information please ring 01545 560 822.

NEW QUAY HONEY FARM, CROSS INN, NEW QUAY, CEREDIGION SA44 6NN

THE CROWN INN & RESTAURANT
LLWYNDAFYDD • TEL: (01545) 560396
(Between New Quay & Cwmtydu)

Open 7 days 12–3pm, 6–11pm
(Sundays 12–3pm, 6–10.30pm)
★ Sunday Lunches 12–2pm-*Bookings Advisable*
★ Home Cooking with local fresh fish
and meat our speciality
★ Brewmasters Standards Award
Also featured in Egon Ronay Guide and
Which's Guide to Country Pubs
★ Restaurant-À la carte Menu-*Bookings Advisable*
Bar Meals 12–2pm and 6–9.15pm

harbour and enjoy the panoramic views across Cardigan Bay, or take a boat trip and explore the bay from an entirely different perspective. Activities off the water include superb coastal walks to Llanina Point, where the tiny church of St. Ina is perched precariously on the cliff top, and to the sandy beach of Cei Bach in Little Quay Bay.

During the 1940's, the great Welsh writer and poet Dylan Thomas lived in New Quay. Many claim that the village is the "cliff-perched town at the far end of Wales" on which he based the fictional Llareggub in Under Milk Wood - a fact hotly disputed by the estuary town of Laugharne, in Carmarthenshire, Dylan's home at the time of his death in New York in 1953.

To the west of New Quay's narrow terraced streets rises the 300-ft summit of New Quay Head, one of the most distinctive landmarks of Cardigan Bay. Two interesting features along its rocky cliffs are Ogof

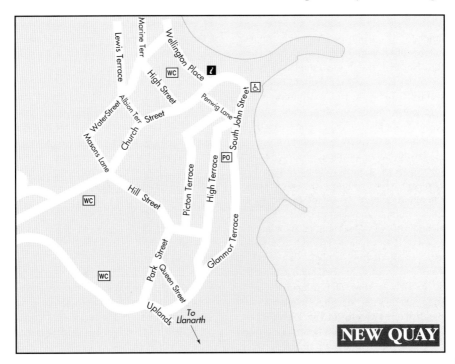

NEW QUAY

New Quay

was to remain unfulfilled. But the boom in coastal trading saw a sudden explosion in shipbuilding. In began around 1820, boosted in 1835 when the current pier was built, using stone quarried locally from the cliff top above Ogo'r Ffeirad (Parson's Cave) and transported to the harbour by tram. By the 1860's the town had 300 shipwrights, supported by several smithies producing anchors, stanchions and other fittings. Most of the hardwood was obtained locally and softwoods came from Canada.

These were prosperous days - but short lived. First the horizon was darkened for wooden boatbuilders by the arrival of iron-built steamships, followed quickly by railways and road transport. However, the old harbour dues displayed at New Quay are a reminder of that rich age. To land a billiard table cost five shillings, but a pig could come ashore for only four pence!

Avoiding any sort of duties - and the customs man - was the work of smugglers, who in the 18th century took full advantage of the miles of secluded coves and hidden caves around New Quay to secrete their ill-gotten hoards of brandy, tobacco, tea, wines and salt.

New Quay today is still well known for its fishing, as shown by the lobster pots which line the quayside and local boats selling their freshly-caught fish. Pollack provide an attractive catch for shore anglers. New Quay also has a lifeboat station, which is open to visitors in summer.

Llanarth Garden Centre & Model Village, near New Quay Located just 2 miles from New Quay, Llanarth Garden Centre has been well established for several years. A recent attraction, however, is the model village, which opened in the summer of 1994. It currently comprises about 50 models and covers in the region of an acre, and is laid out within beautiful gardens which are themselves a delight to walk

Ddauben (the two-headed cave - so called because it has two entrances) and Craig-y-Adar (Bird's Rock) which attracts large numbers of seabirds. A much smaller number of birds find their way to New Quay Bird Hospital, which was established in the 1970's to clean and rehabilitate oil-coated seabirds. Today it treats all injured and damaged wildlife, including seals, and the hospital is open to visitors and welcomes contributions to aid its invaluable work.

Historically speaking, New Quay is something of a rarity along the coast of Cardigan Bay. Many of the earlier communities here date back to the age of Celtic saints and before, but the first mention of New Quay was in an Admiralty report of 1748 which described it as a hamlet with small fishing sloops. It certainly developed as a fishing port, taking advantage of the rich pickings of Cardigan Bay with large catches of herring, mackerel and shellfish. By the turn of the 19th century, New Quay had designs on becoming a major ferry port for Ireland - an ambition which around. For more information ring 01545 580271.

Llanarth Pottery, near New Quay Watch the potter at work and browse through the large showroom, home of the biggest collection of handthrown stoneware pots in Wales. Children and disabled visitors are welcome; there is ample room for wheelchairs.

New Quay Bird Hospital The hospital is a life-saver for animals and birds which have been injured, and it specialises in the treatment of seals and oiled seabirds. It is open for conducted tours during summer months. For times and details ring 01545 560462.

Trysordy Cymru, New Quay Overlooking New Quay's 'Dolphin Bay' - the predominantly stone beach known as Traeth

Y Dolau - this interesting shop specialises in quality gifts and crafts made in Wales. There are areas within the shop dedicated to Welsh music and books. The former, available on cassette, includes relaxation and inspirational music. For more information ring 01545 561195.

Penbryn
Lying below the wooded cliffs that extend between Llangrannog and Tresaith is the long, golden beach of Penbryn. Penbryn itself nestles half a mile inland, in the picturesque valley of the little River Hoffnant. The area is very attractive for its cliff walks and beaches, and in summer boasts a great variety of butterflies, such as meadow brown, common skipper, peacock, common blue, tortoise-shell and others. The mysterious hillside church of St. Michael's is thought to be one of the oldest in Wales. Among its many curious features are a weeping chancel, a leper squint and a sacramental cup dated 1574. Legend has it that the walls of the graveyard are circular so that there are no corners for the Devil to hide in, and it is also said that when an attempt was made to rebuild the church on another site, the stones were miraculously returned to this ancient site overnight. Such stories support the idea that the area has been occupied for many centuries. Iron Age and Romano-British remains have been uncovered, and on the cliff top between Penbryn and Tresaith is the remnant of a hillfort. There is also an inscribed standing stone at Dyffryn Bern, a short distance inland, under which was found a gold coin dating from the first century AD and a burial urn. Weapons and bones have also been discovered close by.

Ponterwyd
Close to Devil's Bridge where the River Rheidol emerges from Plynlimon before plunging into the gorge, this village is famous

THE GEORGE BORROW HOTEL PONTERWYD
NR ABERYSTWYTH

WTB 1 STAR COMMENDED

Famous Hotel visited by George Borrow in 1854

Bed and Breakfast £23 p.p.p.n.
All rooms en-suite & double glazed, colour TV, refreshment tray and central heating
Good Home-Cooked Bar Food served lunchtimes and evenings. Restaurant and Sunday Lunch
Beer Garden overlooking Rheidol Gorge
Children Welcome

TEL: (01970) 890230
RESIDENT PROPS: JOHN & JILL WALL

for the George Borrow Hotel. On a chilly night in 1854, while researching his book Wild Wales, the renowned author, traveller and linguist enjoyed the hospitality of this establishment - then a coaching inn known as the Gogerddan Arms, renamed in his honour earlier this century. The hotel is only 12 miles east of Aberystwyth and is ideally located for exploring the university town and the stunning countryside of Plynlimon and the Rheidol Valley.

Bwlch Nant-yr-Arian Visitor Centre Located just west of Ponterwyd, the Centre stands at the head of a valley and enjoys superb views over the countryside of the Rheidol Forest. Here you can follow the forest trails and learn all about the working woodland and its wildlife and landscape. Kestrels, buzzards and the rare red kites may all be seen in the area. Souvenirs and trail guides are available from the Centre, including a booklet on the Hafod Trail referred to on page 38. For more information ring 01974 261404

Llywernog Silver-Lead Mine This well-known visitor attraction lies on the road between Ponterwyd and Aberystwyth and is just west of the village. The mine is an important reminder that in the 18th and 19th centuries the mining of lead and silver ores was a major industry in the Rheidol Valley and northern Ceredigion. Indeed, in the boom days of the 1860's, Cardiganshire silver was renowned throughout the world. But this award-winning 6-acre site is much more than a history lesson. It provides plenty of fascinating things to see and do and is great fun for children. For example, you can pan for 'gold', silver and gems; try your hand at dowsing for mineral veins; go prospecting for ore; follow the miners' trail past working waterwheels and colourful exhibitions; and have a guided lamplight tour of levels and caverns on the main silver-lead lode, deep

THE RED KITE
Cafe & Restaurant
Opposite Silver Lead Mine, Ponterwyd

● Open 7 days a week ●
● Meals served all day ●
● Pool Table/Gifts ●
● Secondhand Books ●
● Fully Licensed ●

Tel: 01970 890229

Dyffryn Castell
WTB ★★ **Hotel** AA

Situated in the tranquil Cambrian Mountains, 20 minutes from the coastal town of Aberystwyth. This family run hotel offers en suite accommodation with colour TV and beverage facilities in all bedrooms. Cosy bars with real ale and home cooked food with ample choices. Sunday Lunches, Welsh Cream Teas. Children welcome. Coaches by prior arrangement.

Ponterwyd, Nr Devils Bridge, Aberystwyth, Ceredigion SY23 3LB. Tel/Fax 01970 890237
Proprietors: Mervyn & Anne Bunton

underground. There is also a tea room and a gift and souvenir shop selling inexpensive minerals, crystals and silver jewellery.

Pontrhydfendigaid
This small riverside village is 4 miles north-east of Tregaron, on the B4343, and just a mile from the ruins of Strata Florida Abbey. The village hosts an important annual eisteddfod. It is held in the large festival hall, which was a gift to the village from the

Tregaron

and since the days of the drovers the town has been an important meeting place for those who make a living from sheep and cattle. Today the scattered farming communities come here for the livestock market, which alternates every week with Lampeter.

As well as being a staging post for drovers, 18th-century Tregaron was also renowned for its stocking fairs. The stockings were made by farmers' wives as a means of supplementing an often meagre income. The town even had its own bank notes, which bore a black sheep and were issued by the Aberystwyth and Tregaron Bank.

Tregaron (which means the town of Caron) reputedly derives its name from a shepherd boy who became King of Ceredigion in the third century. He is buried in the round churchyard of St. Caron, which stands on top of a mound in the centre of the town. The tower of the church dates from the 14th century and one of its walls bears a small inscribed stone from the nearby Roman fort of Bremio. In the mid-19th century the church served as a school during the winter months, but in summer stood empty as the children toiled on the farms.

In the town square is a bronze statue of Henry Richard, one of Tregaron's most famous sons. He was Radical MP for Merthyr Tydfil for 20 years until his death in 1888, and he founded the European Peace Union - forerunner of the League of Nations and the United Nations Organisation. There is a library named after him near the Houses of Parliament which is for the exclusive use of members.

An infamous son of Tregaron was Twm Shon Catti (real name Thomas Jones) - the Robin Hood of Wales. Legend has it that he lived by plundering his neighbours and tricked an heiress into marrying him, thereby amassing a fortune and later achieving the status of High Sheriff of the county.

In the middle of Tregaron you will find

locally-born millionaire Sir David James. A mile to the north of Pontrhydfendigaid, a narrow road leads to the Teifi Pools, to the east of which are the Claerwen Dam and the Elan Valley.

Tregaron

This small and very Welsh market town, 12 miles north-east of Lampeter and close to the source of the Teifi, is the most easterly town in Ceredigion. To the visitor it offers not only a fascinating history, but is also a pony trekking centre and the gateway to a stunningly beautiful landscape and several major attractions. For example, all within easy driving distance are the National Nature Reserve of Cors Caron, the ruins of Strata Florida Abbey, the Teifi Pools, and the vast upland wilderness which stretches 20 miles east to Abergwesyn and which is often described as the great Welsh desert.

Welsh is the first language of Tregaron,

Rhiannon®

THE WELSH GOLD CENTRE, TREGARON, SY25 6JL
TEL - 01974 298415 FAX - 01974 298690

DESIGNER CELTIC JEWELLERY

Although Rhiannon has an international reputation as a designer of original Celtic jewellery, every piece is still made in Tregaron, by Welsh-speaking goldsmiths. In our display workshop and jewellery showroom, you can watch the jewellery being made, and see the whole range of Rhiannon's beautiful designs.

Many of Rhiannon's designs are inspired by Welsh and Celtic legends or mythology, or are derived from studies of local animals and birds - their final pattern and form shaped by a thorough knowledge of the Celtic heritage. This heritage, which arguably belongs to all the historic peoples of Europe, is probably more alive in Wales than anywhere else today.

Rhiannon also designs and makes a special collection of jewellery containing 10% of rare Welsh Gold, mined in north Wales. This special jewellery is only available from The Welsh Gold Centre in Tregaron - if you can't come to visit us, please ask for our mail order catalogue.

THE CELTIC DESIGN CENTRE

In the associated Celtic Design Centre, you will find a wide range of quality hand-made gifts which reflect the rich heritage of Wales and Celtic Britain - everything from unusual souvenirs to future heirlooms! Many are especially commissioned to our own designs, and are not available elsewhere.

Established since 1971, this centre now attracts visitors from across the world looking for Welsh or Celtic products. It also attracts a large regular clientele from Wales itself - a sign perhaps that this is a rather different kind of "Craft Shop".

All the staff are Welsh-speaking, and they have an intimate knowledge of Wales and the Welsh heritage of Ynys Prydain (the Island of Britain).

Follow the unbroken common thread that connects the Celtic Lands through the centuries, interweaving with our language, poetry, music, art and folklore like the intricate knotwork of the great Christian manuscripts - and take home a gift that is worthy of Wales.

www.rhiannon.co.uk

56

Strata Florida Abbey

the Rhiannon Welsh Gold Centre. This specialist craft centre has an international reputation for its unusual range of Welsh and Celtic gifts as well as the renowned Rhiannon silver and gold jewellery, made on the premises.

The great bog of Tregaron, the Cors Caron National Nature Reserve, lies just to the north of the town. At nearly 2,000 acres it is the biggest raised peat bog in Wales (and reputedly the biggest outside Ireland) and is still growing. It is the result of gradual draining of two ancient lakes formed by the damming action of rocks and other debris (known as a moraine) deposited by glaciers in the Ice Age. The infant River Teifi cuts a tortuous course through it, and the bog is a very important site for research, providing a rich variety of habitats for plants, insects, birds and animals. Over 160 species of birds have been seen here, including the red kite, and many species breed on or near the reserve. Among the animals which enjoy its protection and isolation are polecats, otters and mink. The bog is managed by the Nature Conservancy Council, who also own most of it, and entry is by special permit only. There is, however, a public nature trail which follows the course of the disused railway line. At the end of the trail is an observation tower giving views over a wide area of this unique and fascinating bogland.

Also of great interest in the area are the abbey ruins of Strata Florida and the small village of Llanddewibrefi - once Lampeter's rival for the site of St. David's College. From Tregaron, a narrow mountain road heads east through the Cwm Berwyn pass to Abergwesyn. This wonderful scenic drive follows the route of 18th-century drovers heading for the markets of England.

Cors Caron National Nature Reserve Cors Caron is the vast area of raised peat bog lying between Tregaron and Pontrhydfendigaid. It is of great scientific interest and value because of its variety of habitats for plants, insects, birds and animals, and is regarded as the finest example of a living peat bog outside Ireland. Access is limited, though there is a nature trail and observation tower. For more information ring 01974 298480.

Strata Florida Abbey Apart from its magnificent west door - a highly decorated Celtic-Romanesque arch - very little survives of this 12th-century Cistercian abbey near the village of Pontrhydfendigaid, about 7 miles north-east of Tregaron. But in its day it was a centre of great influence and learning, due in no small measure to the astonishing business enterprise of the monks themselves. Not only did they become huge landowners and very successful sheep farmers, with over 1000 sheep on pastures extending from Cardigan Bay inland to Rhayader: they also grew wheat, oats and barley; operated several corn and woollen mills; established a pub

Llyn Brianne Reservoir

selling their own brew; bred trout and eels and were accomplished sea fishermen; mined silver-lead at Cwm Ystwyth; mined and smelted iron ore; built roads and bridges; and became major wool exporters, King John granting them a licence to export to France and Flanders free of duty. In between times they also illustrated manuscripts and encouraged the Welsh language and literature.

The abbey was founded in 1164 when a group of Cistercian monks from Whitland Abbey established a fledgling community here, choosing the site for its serene and peaceful setting. The following year they attracted the patronage of the wealthy Lord Rhys, prince of the ancient kingdom of Deheubarth, and in time work began on building the new Strata Florida Abbey - 'the Westminster of Wales'. Much of the stone came by sea from Somerset and had to be hauled overland from Cardigan Bay.

It is said that pilgrims and the sick came here to see the abbey's most treasured possession - a wooden cup thought to be the Holy Grail (a chalice used at the Last Supper) and which supposedly had great healing powers. Other visitors to Strata Florida were the Welsh princes, who gathered here in 1238 to swear allegiance to Dafydd, son of Llywelyn the Great.

Life at the abbey was not without its disasters. In 1286 the church was struck by lightning and burned to the ground; in 1295 royalist forces set fire to the abbey and caused significant damage; and in 1348-49 the monks' numbers were reduced by the Black Death.

Strata Florida Abbey closed in 1539 with the Dissolution of the Monasteries under Henry VIII. Many of the last native Welsh princes are buried here, and a gnarled yew tree in the adjoining churchyard is said to mark the grave of the great medieval Welsh poet Dafydd ap Gwilym. The abbey ruins are now under the care of CADW, and there is a small museum on the site. For more information ring CADW on 01222 500200

Tregaron Harness Racing A centuries-old sport dating back to the Romans, harness racing is a popular summer attraction at the Tregaron Trotting Club. The Club's harness races were established in 1984 and are among the best-patronised rural grasstrack events in Wales. The races are held in May and August on the Dol-yr-Ychain racetrack, attracting top-class horses from all over Britain. For more information ring 01974 261343.

Tregaron Pottery Situated 3 miles north-west of Tregaron, on the A485 at Castell Flemish, Tregaron Pottery produces a large range of attractive stoneware in a variety of subtle colours.

Tresaith

Beautiful Tresaith combines the attractions of a superb beach with the magnificent cliff scenery and walks of the Ceredigion Heritage Coast. Noted for its unusual waterfall - formed when the River Saith was diverted over the cliffs during the last Ice Age - Tresaith also enjoys the luxury of having the golden sands of Penbryn and Llangrannog as near neighbours. Beyond the

Tresaith

waterfall are some interesting and dramatic rock structures, including caves, stacks and a deep vertical fissure known as the Devil's Cut. In the 19th century, limestone was brought ashore at Tresaith and roasted in two kilns adjacent to the beach. These kilns also served local farmers who used lime as fertiliser for the poor acidic clay soils.

Wallog

Wallog is a small coastal settlement north of Aberystwyth, on the Clarach-Borth section of the Ceredigion Heritage Coast. There is an old limekiln on the beach, but Wallog's claim to fame is the remarkable ridge of shingle known as Sarn Cynfelin. The ridge, about 60 feet wide, projects from the shore roughly at right angles and extends into the sea for approximately 7 miles. This underwater peninsula, the cause of many shipwrecks in the past, is believed to be the result of glacial deposits of pebbles and boulders from the last Ice Age. Welsh legend, however, has a much more colourful explanation. Sarn Cynfelin was one of the causeways serving the 16 cities of the lost land of Cantre'r Gwaelod (the 'Lowland Hundred'), which stood on a fertile coastal plain now lying beneath the waters of Cardigan Bay. The cities were protected from the sea by dikes and sluices, but one night after a great feast the drunken keeper forgot to close the sluices and Cantre'r Gwaelod was lost beneath the waves. The story goes that sailors have since seen the walls of great palaces shimmering in the sea, or heard the watery chimes of The Bells of Aberdovey. The legend does have a fraction of credibility, as Cardigan Bay was a fertile plain before rising sea levels swamped it. Whatever its origins, Sarn Cynfelin is a very significant landform feature of the bay.

Ynyslas

See the entry under Borth & Ynyslas on page 27.

The Great Sporting & Activity Holiday

Fifty miles of coastline ensures that Ceredigion is a natural centre for sailing and just about every other kind of watersport. But if you prefer your activity holiday to be on dry land, you won't be disappointed. The region's wide choice of sporting and leisure facilities means that you can participate in bowls, clay pigeon shooting, freshwater and sea angling, golf, indoor sports, outdoor pursuits, pony trekking and riding, squash, tennis, cycling, walking, ski-ing and much more.

The following is a guide to the many facilities available, listed alphabetically by sport. Further details are obtainable from the Tourist Information Centres listed on page 81.

Angling (freshwater)

There are many opportunities for freshwater anglers in Ceredigion. For details of venues, clubs, associations, permits, rod licences, fees and so on, contact any Tourist Information Centre.

Angling (sea)

Charter boats operating from Aberystwyth harbour offer a choice of deep-sea and inshore fishing trips, from an hour's mackerel fishing to 12 hours at sea. All boats are fully licensed and insured.

Pleasure trips along the scenic coastline are also popular, particularly with wildlife and birdwatching enthusiasts. Details of all fishing and pleasure trips are advertised at Aberystwyth harbour. Or ring Aberystwyth TIC on 01970 612125 for more information about individual boats and how to contact their skippers direct.

Bowls

Clubs at all the following locations welcome visitors and non-members: Aberaeron, Aberystwyth (Queen's Road), Aberystwyth (Plascrug), Cardigan, Lampeter, Llandysul, Newcastle Emlyn, New Quay and Tregaron.

Clay Pigeon Shooting

For details of clay pigeon shooting at Castell Howell Holiday Centre, near Llandysul, ring 01545 590209.

Cycling

A wide range of bikes and accessories is available for hire from Red Dragon Cycle Services. Ring 01970 880397.

Golf Courses

The courses available to visitors and non-members in Ceredigion are as listed below. You can also take advantage of the new Mid Wales Golf Card, which gives 7 days' unlimited golf on a variety of courses in the region. For details ring 01938 553631.

Aberaeron A 9-hole pitch and putt course at Drefach Farm, just north of Aberaeron, overlooking Cardigan Bay. Fees include all equipment, and there is also a crazy golf course. Ring 01545 570329. Aberystwyth An 18-hole course the town with panoramic views over Cardigan Bay. Clubhouse, full catering facilities, club professional and shop. Visitors welcome. Ring 01970 615104.

Aberdovey An 18 hole, par 71 course and Ian Woosnam's spiritual home. The course wends a traditional route out and back, with sand dunes as sentinels and the wind as friend as foe. Ring 01970 615104

Borth & Ynyslas A leading 18-hole course in Wales and the oldest in the principality, established in 1885, this is one of the championship venues chosen by both the WGU and WLGU. A natural links course adjoining Borth beach, it hosts a series of annual opens in June and is laid out on traditional lines, the holes running out and back across a narrow tract of land. The opening and closing holes are exposed, ensuring a testing start and finish, particularly in the wind. Other challenges are thrown up by the variety of humps, hollows and subtle contours. The modern clubhouse, built in 1992, offers full bar and catering facilities for members and visitors. New members are always welcome (no joining fee) and beginners' courses are held in spring. Visitors are also warmly welcomed on payment of green fees. Ring 01970 871202.

Capel Bangor, Near Aberystwyth Previously known as Cwm Nant, this 9-hole course is set in glorious countryside just off the A44 at Capel Bangor, 4 miles east of Aberystwyth. You pay as you play and club hire is available. Ideal for visitors and occasional golfers, it is open from 9.00 am till dusk. Ring 01970 880239.

Cardigan An 18-hole course at Gwbert-on-Sea, just north of the town. Bar and catering facilities, and squash club with 3 courts. Ring 01239 621775.

Cilgwyn, Near Lampeter Opened in 1977, this now rates among the best 9-hole parkland courses, with clubhouse, bar, meals and shop. Ring 01570 45286.

Cwmrhydneuadd, Near Llangrannog A 9-hole par 31 course just off the A487, close to Llangrannog. It features 3 lakes and measures 1,788 yards, with a particularly challenging final hole. There is a fully-licensed bar and a taste of home cooking. Fly fishing from the well-stocked lakes is an alternative (or additional) activity available here. Ring 01239 654933.

Gwbert-on-Sea, Near Cardigan A 9-hole course at The Cliff Hotel, open to visitors. Ring 01239 613241.

Penlanlas, Near Aberystwyth Opened in 1993, this 9-hole course is situated 4 miles south of Aberystwyth and signposted off the A487 at Rhydyfelin. Alternative tees are in use for second-time rounders, and many holes now include water hazards. It is a challenging course in a spectacular location, with superb views over the Ystwyth Valley and beyond. The golf shop is well stocked and offers realistic prices. The course is open from 9.00am till dusk and visitors are welcome, with discounts for groups of 10 or more. For more information ring 01970 625319.

Penrhos Golf & Country Club, Llanrhystud A superb new 18-hole championship course which opened in 1991, with a challenging variety of holes and terrain and spectacular views over Cardigan Bay. Situated on the A487, 7 miles north of Aberaeron and 9 miles south of Aberystwyth, the club's golf and leisure facilities are first-class in every respect and include practice range, clubhouse with bars and restaurant areas, changing rooms, showers, club professional and well-stocked shop, indoor swimming pool, jacuzzi, solarium, steam room, sauna, gymnasium, pool room and kiddies' room. Adjacent to the club is Penrhos Holiday Park, where accommodation is available for a complete golfing holiday. Ring 01974 202999/202236/202238/202254.

Health Clubs

The following all offer health and fitness facilities:

Cardigan Sports Complex (01239 613632)

Glan-y-Mor Leisure Park, Clarach (01970 828900)

Hotel Penrallt, Aberporth (01239 810227)

Ty Hen Farm Hotel, near New Quay (01545 560346)

Outdoor Pursuits

Cardigan Bay 4x4 Quad Trekking Centre
This offers a fun and exciting way for all the family to see the countryside and enjoy spectacular views over New Quay and Cardigan Bay. Located near the village of Llwyncelyn, just half a mile off the A487 between New Quay and Aberaeron, the Centre provides full pre-trek instruction on how to handle a quad bike - a machine which is great fun even for inexperienced riders. There is a choice of treks over 500 acres of working farmland, embracing open fields, farm tracks and woodland. Safety is paramount: helmets and waterproof clothing are provided and qualified instructors are on hand at all times. The bikes are suitable for everyone aged 13 and over, and the Centre is open 7 days a week throughout the year. For more information ring 01545 580385.

Diffwys Outdoor Pursuits Centre
Located at Cwm Berwyn, near Tregaron, this offers tuition to groups on rock climbing, canoeing, abseiling, hill walking and archery. Horse riding and mountain biking are available by prior arrangement. Ring 01974 298496.

Pony Trekking and Riding

There is a good choice of pony trekking and riding establishments throughout Ceredigion. Here are a few to get you in the saddle; a full list is available from Tourist Information Centres.

Cardigan Bay Riding Centre, Aberarth (01545 571181)

Castellan Riding Academy, Boncath (01239 841644)

Castell Howell , Llandysul (01545 590209)

Cefn Faes Farm, near Tregaron (01974 821447)

Dyfed Riding Centre, near Cardigan (01239 612594 day or 613159 evening)

Plas-y-Wern Riding Stables, New Quay (01545 580156)

Rheidol Riding Centre, Aberystwyth (01970 880863)

Sailing, Yachting and Rowing Clubs

Aberaeron Yacht Club (01545 570077)

Aberporth Sailing & Boating Club (01239 810238)

Aberystwyth Boat Club 01970 624575

Llangrannog Boating & Angling Association (01239 654459)

New Quay Yacht Club (01545 560516/560037)

Teifi Boating Club, Cardigan (01239 612361)

Tresaith Mariners Sailing Club (01239 810232)

Ski-ing

Llangrannog Ski Centre is a dry ski slope within the holiday centre of the Welsh League of Youth, close to Llangrannog village and with superb views over Cardigan Bay. The 100-metre slope boasts modern uplift and water mist lubrication systems and caters for all abilities, including absolute beginners. The centre is open all year round and offers discounts to family groups (of 4 or more) and other groups and parties. Ring 01239 654656.

Soccer

Ian Rush International Soccer Tournament This major international youth soccer tournament is one of the biggest events in the Welsh sporting calendar, and is also rated as the best youth competition in Europe. Hosted on the superb playing fields of the University of Wales in Aberystwyth, the tournament attracts teams of boys and girls from around the world, as well as clubs of the calibre of Liverpool, Aston Villa and many others. The tournament is organised into age groups. Boys compete at Under 12, U13, U14, U16 and U18, while girls' competitions are for U14 and U16. Admission for spectators to any particular match is modest, and with the skill factor very high the tournament provides excellent evening entertainment. For more information contact Colin Mitchell, PO Box 30, Welshpool, Powys SY21 9ZZ (ring 01938 553631).

Sports and leisure centres

Cardigan Sports Complex
(01239 613632)
Castell Howell Holiday Centre, Llandysul
(01545 590209)
Lampeter Leisure Centre
(01570 422552)
Newcastle Emlyn Leisure Centre
(01239 711025)
Penglais Sports Centre, Aberystwyth
(01970 615303)
Plascrug Leisure Centre, Aberystwyth
(01970 624579)
Teifi Leisure Centre, Cardigan
(01239 621287)
Tregaron Leisure Centre, Tregaron
(01974 298960)
Ty Hen Farm Hotel, near New Quay
(01545 560364)

Lampeter Leisure Centre

- Multi-purpose Hall
- Fitness Suite
- Conference Room
- Aerobics
- Trampolining
- Netball
- Badminton
- Basketball

Children's Activities include -
Saturday Roller Disco,
Birthday Parties, plus
Holiday Activities

FOR FUTHER DETAILS TELEPHONE
01570 422552

Swimming Pools (indoor)
Aberaeron (01545 570871)
Aberystwyth (01970 624579)
Cardigan (01239 613632)
Castell Howell Holiday Centre, Llandysul (01545 590209)
Llandysul (01559 352548)
Newcastle Emlyn (01239 710122)
Tregaron (01974 298231)
Ty Hen Farm Hotel, near New Quay (01545 560346)

Tennis
There are clubs in Aberaeron, Aberystwyth, Borth, Cardigan and New Quay which welcome visitors and non-members. There is also indoor tennis at the Penglais Sports Centre in Aberystwyth, and an all-weather court at Castell Howell, Llandysul.

On offer at your local leisure centre . . .

CARON
LEISURE CENTRE

A full range of sports and leisure facilities with daily activities during all holiday periods. Starting at 1pm with our **FAMILY FUN HOUR** followed by **FUN & GAMES** *for the over 7's* Aerobics, Step & Slide, Squash, Table Tennis, Badmington, Fitness Suite and Archery
Junior activities: Karate, Judo, Gymnastics with Bouncy Castle Saturday mornings - and Roller Disco in the afternoon
FOR FURTHER DETAILS TELEPHONE
KEVIN DOYLE ON (01974) 298960
CARON LEISURE CENTRE, CARDIGANSHIRE

• Health & Fitness classes

• Roller Skating

• Childrens Parties

• Martial Arts classes

• Superb Fitness Suite

• Badminton

• Solarium

• Childrens Holiday Activities

and much much more for all the family

Open 7 days a week

Canolfan Hamdden — Teifi — Leisure Centre

CARDIGAN
☎ **(01239) 621287**

The Great Sporting & Activity Holiday

- Swimming Pool
- Squash Courts
- Badminton Courts
- Sports Hall
- Learner Pool
- Fitness Suite
- Solarium
- Whirlpool Spa
- Sauna
- Bar & Catering
- Outside Tennis Courts

I'r teulu gyfan
For all the family

Canolfan Hamdden

PLASCRUG
Leisure Centre

Aberystwyth
☎**(01970) 624579**

Cardigan Swimming Pool & Leisure Complex

Did **you** *know you have nearly* **all** *the Leisure Facility in Cardigan under* **one** *roof?*

YES

Two *swimming pools, Sports Hall,* **Superb** *Fitness Suite, Solarium, Sauna & Lounge*

Fairground, Cardigan SA43 1AJ
Tel: 01239 613632/613056

Walking

Walk packs, with maps and detailed guidance notes, are available from Tourist Information Centres and some retailers throughout Ceredigion. The walks they cover include the Rheidol Valley near Aberystwyth, Cardigan and the Teifi Valley. For details, ring Aberystwyth TIC on 01970 612125.

In addition, various groups of the Ramblers Association meet and walk regularly.

The Lampeter Group, for example, holds a series of walks in the district during the year, and welcomes visitors and new members.

The Aberystwyth Group holds regular walks which vary from 5 to 11 miles and are graded easy, moderate or strenuous.

The Cardigan Group also makes regular walks, of varied length, from supplied grid references.

Aberystwyth Ramblers (01970 828565)
Cardigan Ramblers (01239 711057)
Lampeter Ramblers (01570 480041)

Windsurfing

Windsurfers, surf skis and surf boards are for sale and hire at Borth. There is also expert tuition by Peter Hunt, a former member of the British Windsurfing Team. Ring 01970 828584.

The magnificent neo-classical building of the National Library of Wales dominates the hillside overlooking the coastline and town of Aberystwyth. The views from its gardens are spectacular. But a much wider view of Wales, and an insight into its people, history and culture, comes from inside the library itself. For here is a vast and priceless collection of books, manuscripts, maps, pictures, letters, public records and many other items which represent a nation's heritage. It is a colossal treasure trove, in which all aspects of the Welsh people and the Welsh way of life are richly expressed and preserved.

Such a collection has established the National Library as the premier cultural and resource centre of Wales. It is a mecca for researchers, and many of its visitors are students and academics delving into areas of Welsh and Celtic studies. Yet Joe Public need not feel excluded, because although this is not a lending library - every item here is strictly for reference - the National Library is open six days a week and has Reading Rooms, a cafe, attractive gardens, a fascinating permanent exhibition, and a variety of invaluable services to offer.

The most popular of these services, and the one most widely used by non-academics, is the provision of genealogical information. An increasing number of people the world over share a fascination for compiling the family tree. In the process, many of them discover Welsh connections and ancestors, and the trail leads to the National Library of Wales. For a sensible charge the library will carry out a search of its very extensive public records and other sources, drawn from parishes all over Wales. Requests for searches can be made in person or by post. The library also produces an interesting and informative pamphlet entitled A Guide to Genealogical Sources At the National Library of Wales, which is available free on request.

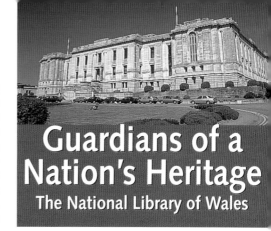

Guardians of a Nation's Heritage
The National Library of Wales

Popular with visitors are the various exhibitions staged in the library's galleries. These vary from the permanent exhibition, A Nation's Heritage, to the temporary exhibitions featuring many of Wales' leading artists and photographers, past and present. For a behind-the-scenes look at the work of the institution, ask to see the library's video showing in the Gregynog Gallery.

If you wish to indulge in some serious reading, and can produce proof of identity, you can also gain access to the Reading Rooms. At your disposal will be the 5 million books currently in the library's care. Every year another 300,000 are added by virtue of the library's copyright status (it is one of only 5 legal deposit libraries in Britain), which enables it to claim one copy of every book, periodical, newspaper, map and piece of music published in the UK. To accommodate the increasing number of books published and to provide ideal storage conditions for rare material, a new £11 million extension to the library has recently been completed. The Third Library Building was officially opened by Queen Elizabeth II in May 1996 and should provide sufficient storage space for the library to expand for the next twenty years.

Books are not the only thing you can look at. The library's Department of Pictures & Maps is one of Britain's largest cartographical resources and can show you everything from contemporary and historical Welsh maps to town plans, tithe maps, railway plans and sea charts. There are also about 500,000 photographs of Welsh interest - the largest and richest collection in existence. And in addition to its parish registers, the Department of Manuscripts & Records has literary and personal papers of Welsh and Anglo-Welsh writers, artists, scholars and politicians, including Lloyd George and Augustus John. Since 1980 it has also collected visual and audio-visual material, and the many papers in the Political Archive are now supplemented by radio and TV news broadcasts and current affairs programmes.

Another bonus for researchers is that much of the material within the library's charge, including photographs, can be supplied as facsimile copies, subject to the limitations of the Copyright Act.

The National Library of Wales was established by Royal Charter in 1907. The foundation stones were laid in 1911 by King George V and Queen Mary, and when it was officially opened in 1937 by King George VI and Queen Elizabeth - the present Queen Mother - it was already well established and had acquired many of the treasures described here.

Today, the library's collection continues to grow through deposit, gift, purchase and exchange. Maybe a library is not an obvious holiday attraction. But then, this is no ordinary library, and many of the people who come here leave with the feeling that to have missed the National Library of Wales would be to miss the very heart and soul of the principality.

Llyfrgell Genedlaethol Cymru

The National Library of Wales

Trysorfa Cenedl

Dewch i weld trysorau'r Llyfrgell sy'n rhan o'r arddangosfa barhaol ac hefyd i fwynhau amrywiaeth o arddangosfeydd teithiol mewn adeilad gwych. Y cyfan am ddim.

Am fanylion pellach cysylltwch â'r Uned Farchnata
☎ **(01970) 632800**

A Nation's Heritage

Come and see the Library's treasures on show in the permanent exhibition and enjoy a variety of touring exhibitions housed in an impressive building. All free of charge.

For further details contact the Marketing Unit
☎ **(01970) 632800**

Aberystwyth, Ceredigion, SY23 3BU
Cymru / Wales U.K.

South Teifi

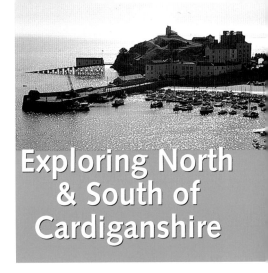

Exploring North & South of Cardiganshire

High in the hills above the ruins of Strata Florida Abbey, a small stream trickles tentatively from a deep pool known as Llyn Teifi. Seventy miles later it gushes out into Cardigan Bay between Gwbert-on-Sea and Poppit Sands. This is the River Teifi, one of the loveliest rivers in Britain. To the north of it lies Ceredigion, and to the south are Pembrokeshire and Carmarthenshire. .

Pembrokeshire

Pembrokeshire, a beautifully unspoilt peninsula of golden beaches and magnificent cliff scenery, is well known for many things. The Pembrokeshire Coast National Park - one of three in Wales - is the only national park in Britain which is predominantly coastal. The park, remarkably diverse, also embraces the wild Preseli Hills, the tranquil tidal creeks of the Daugleddau estuary and the very picturesque Gwaun Valley.

Pembrokeshire's beaches are among Britain's finest, and in 1998 no less than 25 won important awards including 4 blue flags. Resorts such as Tenby, Saundersfoot, Broad Haven(south and west), Whitesands Bay and Newport Sands have all established the county as a favourite destination for traditional seaside holidays.

Off the beach, Pembrokeshire has many attractions. Medieval castles can be explored at Pembroke, Manorbier and Carew, and older still is the site occupied by St. David's Cathedral, in Britain's smallest city.

The county's many leisure, wildlife and country parks include Oakwood - the biggest and best-known theme park in Wales.

And there are first-class facilities for golf, fishing, watersports and countless other sports and activities. For walkers there is the challenge of the 186-mile Pembrokeshire Coast Path.

The following is a very brief guide (in alphabetical order) to just a few of the hundreds of attractions and places of interest to be discovered in Pembrokeshire. All those listed are within easy driving distance of Cardigan.

Castell Henllys Iron Age Fort This remarkable and archaeologically-important example of an Iron Age fort is managed by the National Park Authority and has been partially reconstructed with thatched roundhouses, animal pens, a smithy and a grain store, all standing on their original sites. For further information ring 01239 79319.

Dyfed Shire Horse Farm, Eglwyswrw Carnhuan Farm was the lifelong home of the late and distinguished shire horse breeder John Rees Lewis. Attractions include show horses, harnesses, a daily parade, horse and wagon rides, pony rides, farm history and exhibitions, demonstrations, and opportunities to feed the farm's many other animals. For more information ring 01834 891640.

Oakwood Oakwood has also developed as a major entertainment centre in West Wales. For more information about Oakwood's ever-growing number of great attractions, ring 01834 891373.

St David's Cathedral

SHIRE HORSE
DYFED FARM

- Talk on Shire Horses
- Harnessing demonstrations
- Picnic areas (indoors/outdoors)
- Bottle Feeding
- 1.15pm only:~
  Duke in splendid
  show harness
- Play areas (indoors/outdoors)
- Working horses
- Horse/wagon rides
- Tractor/trailer tours
- Craft demonstrations
- History & Video rooms
- Harness/Craft rooms
- Gift shop/Cafe
- Pony rides (supervised)

OPEN Good Friday April 16 to May 30 - June 4 daily; June 5 - June 25 daily except Sats, Suns, Mons; June26 - July 16 daily except Sats, Suns; July 17 - Sept 3 daily except Sats; Sept 4 - Oct 1 open Weds & Thurs only. Also Xmas Santa Specials - phone for details.

CARNHUAN, NEAR EGLWYSWRW,CARDIGAN SA41 3SY
TELEPHONE: 01834 891640 or 01239891253
on A487 nr junction B4329 3/4 mile south of
Eglwyswrw, Cardigan to Fishguard road

St. David's Cathedral & the Bishop's Palace It was in the 6th century that St. David, the patron saint of Wales, established a semi-monastic religious settlement on this sheltered site in the valley of the little River Alun. Centuries later, after frequent pillaging and destruction of the early churches by Viking raiders, the cathedral as it stands today began to take shape. This was in 1180, and the builder was Peter de Leia, the third Norman bishop. The cathedral was completed in 1522. It is the largest church in Wales, and certainly the most interesting. The total interior length is nearly 300 feet and the tower is 125 ft high: small by comparison with cathedrals on the grand scale of York Minster, but for centuries a mighty inspiration to the Welsh.

Following the Reformation the cathedral was neglected, and severe damage was inflicted in the Civil War. In 1862 Sir George Gilbert Scott was commissioned to begin a complete restoration of the cathedral, the work continuing into this century. In 1866, during the restoration, the bones of two men were found in a recess which had been walled up. It is believed that these were the remains of St. David and his friend and teacher St. Justinian, and the bones are now contained in an oak chest in the Holy Trinity chapel. Other tombs in the cathedral include those of Bishop Gower, Edmund Tudor - father of Henry VII - and Giraldus Cambrensis (Gerald of Wales).

St. David's Cathedral is open to visitors every day. Among the many events hosted here are concerts of the St. David's and Fishguard music festivals.

St. Dogmael's Abbey Across the Teifi estuary from Cardigan is the picturesque fishing village of St. Dogmael's and the remains of the 12th-century abbey. It was built in 1115 by Benedictine monks from France - a replacement for an earlier Celtic monastery which had stood on the site until Viking raiders destroyed it in the 10th century. The north and west walls of the nave are still standing.

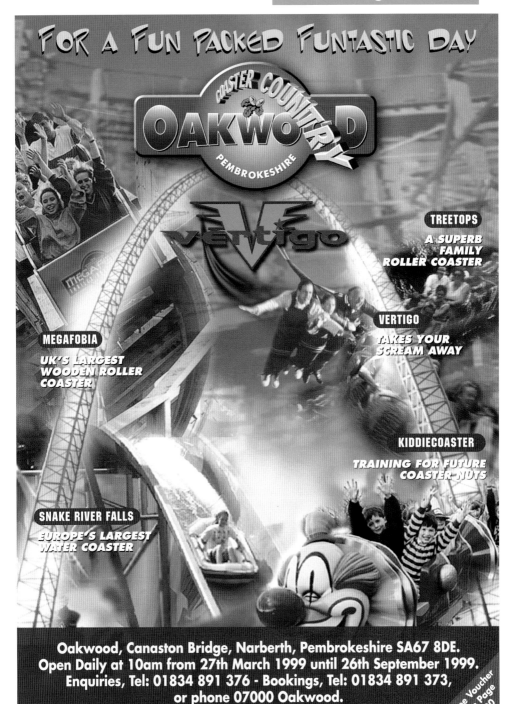

FOR A FUN PACKED FUNTASTIC DAY

COASTER COUNTRY
OAKWOOD
PEMBROKESHIRE

VERTIGO

TREETOPS
A SUPERB
FAMILY
ROLLER COASTER

MEGAFOBIA
UK'S LARGEST
WOODEN ROLLER
COASTER

VERTIGO
TAKES YOUR
SCREAM AWAY

KIDDIECOASTER
TRAINING FOR FUTURE
COASTER NUTS

SNAKE RIVER FALLS
EUROPE'S LARGEST
WATER COASTER

Oakwood, Canaston Bridge, Narberth, Pembrokeshire SA67 8DE.
Open Daily at 10am from 27th March 1999 until 26th September 1999.
Enquiries, Tel: 01834 891 376 - Bookings, Tel: 01834 891 373,
or phone 07000 Oakwood.

See Voucher
on Page
80

Carmarthenshire

Carmarthenshire is a very attractive holiday destination for visitors who appreciate history, culture and a green and beautiful environment. Covering an area of 1,000 square miles, the county is a veritable feast of delights and discovery - an intoxicating mix of glorious coast and countryside, offering a wealth of activities.

The 50 miles of stunning coastline embrace vast stretches of safe golden sands, such as the beaches of Cefn Sidan and Pendine, punctuated by the Taf and Towy estuaries, which so inspired Dylan Thomas. The Loughor estuary, a favourite haunt of migratory birds, is famous for its cockles - a delicacy to be found in the markets of Llanelli and Carmarthen.

The unspoilt and contrasting countryside of Carmarthenshire touches the edge of the Brecon Beacons National Park in the east, the Cambrian mountains in the north and the picturesque Teifi Valley to the west.

The county is also rich in bustling market towns, such as Newcastle Emlyn, Whitland, Llandeilo, Llandovery and Carmarthen.

And the attractions and activities to be enjoyed in Carmarthenshire are many and varied - from castles, museums and art galleries to steam railways, country parks, fishing and golf.

Carmarthen At the heart of the county is the ancient township of Carmarthen. It stands on the River Towy, 8 miles inland – a position which inspired the Romans to make it their strategic regional capital. They also built an amphitheatre here, rediscovered in 1936 but first excavated in 1968. In legend, the town is the reputed birthplace of Merlin – wizard and counsellor to King Arthur.

Today, Carmarthen's quaint old narrow streets are full of Welsh character and tradition. There's also a first-class modern shopping centre with many familiar High Street names, complemented by Carmarthen's famous market. Open six days a week, the market attracts people from all over Wales. The colourful atmosphere is enriched by the banter and barter of the adjacent livestock mart – Wales' biggest. You're also likely to catch more than a smattering of Welsh, as it is still widely spoken here. It is believed that the oldest manuscript in the Welsh language – The Black Book of Carmarthen, now in the National Library of Wales in Aberystwyth – was written in the town.

Carmarthen Bay South of Carmarthen, the River Towy emerges into Carmarthen Bay alongside the rivers Taf and Gwendraeth. This is an area of outstanding natural beauty, where scores of waders and seabirds take rich pickings from the broad expanse of mudflats formed by the three estuaries.

Here too you will discover the charming seaside villages of Ferryside and Llansteffan, at the mouth of the Towy. Just a short hop west to the Taf estuary takes you to Laugharne – a medieval township where the great poet and writer Dylan Thomas spent the latter years of his tragically short life. His home was the Boat House – his "seashaken house on a breakneck of rocks", standing above the estuary – which is now a Heritage

Laugharne

MUSEUM OF THE WELSH WOOLLEN INDUSTRY
Dre-fach Felindre

A working mill with demonstrations of traditional hand carding, spinning, and weaving. Extensive range of quality Welsh crafts to buy. Facilities include a cafe, a museum shop selling traditional fabrics and merchandise, a working woollen mill, craft workshops, a riverside picnic area, factory trails and free parking. There are also disabled facilities and ground floor access.

Tel: (01559) 370 929

—— THE NATIONAL ——
CORACLE CENTRE
AND FLOUR MILL
CENARTH FALLS
NEWCASTLE EMLYN, CARMARTHENSHIRE

A unique display of coracles from Wales and around the world set in the grounds of the 17th Century Flour Mill

—— OPEN ——

Easter – October Sun – Fri 10.30am – 5.30pm
and at other times by appointment

Telephone Martin Fowler on:
01239 710980 or 710507

Centre dedicated to his memory.

From Laugharne, the road west cuts a picturesque route to Pendine Sands, where Sir Malcolm Campbell and others made several attempts on the world landspeed record. The fatal crash of Parry Thomas-Jones in 1927 ended Pendine's racing career, but the exciting new Museum of Speed recalls this village resort's days of fame and glory.

On the eastern side of Carmarthen Bay are the estuaries of the Gwendraeth and Loughour, and the superb seven-mile beach of Cefn Sidan Sands - one of the best beaches in Britain.

Castles Carmarthenshire boasts several outstanding examples of Norman castles. One of the best-preserved medieval fortresses in Wales is Kidwelly Castle, while the imposing ruins at Carreg Cennen and Llansteffan both enjoy spectacular elevated positions. And Laugharne Castle, where Dylan Thomas wrote Portrait of the Artist as a Young Dog, has been extensively refurbished by Cadw (Welsh Historic Monuments) and is now open to visitors. Dinefwr Castle, near Llandeilo, is another sight not to be missed.

Attractions in the Teifi Valley The Teifi Valley is rich in rural traditions and customs. There are also many attractions and beauty spots nestling alongside the river's winding course, some of which are described here.

Teifi Valley Railway A short but very enjoyable journey by narrow gauge railway into the beautiful Teifi Valley is the pleasure awaiting you at Henllan Station, between Newcastle Emlyn and Llandysul. New for 1998 is a 1/4 mile Ride on a Miniature Railway, A delightful 20 minute experience for all ages. For timetable and other enquiries ring 01559 371077.

Cenarth Cenarth is one of the most popular beauty spots in the whole of West Wales. It stands on the River Teifi and is a very pretty village, famous for its salmon-leap falls. It is also recognised as the traditional home of the Teifi coracle, and here you will find the National Coracle Centre, which despite its name is a private enterprise, though no less important or interesting for that. Unspoilt Cenarth is a designated conservation area, with many of its buildings listed. The fine old bridge is believed to be 18th century, and the flour mill which houses the Coracle Centre dates from the 1600's. Also of historical interest is St. Llawddog's church and its mysterious Sarsen Stone.

Coracle Centre & Mill, Cenarth The strange, round fishing boat known as the coracle has been a familiar sight on the River Teifi for centuries. It is light, manoeuvrable and ideal in shallow water, though mastering the art of coracle fishing can take years of practice. Today there are still 12 pairs licensed to fish on the Teifi, but the best place to see coracles is here at the National Coracle Centre. The Centre houses over 20 different types of coracle, in varying shapes and sizes, from all over the world – India, Vietnam, Tibet, Iraq and North America – as well as 9 varieties of Welsh coracle and examples from England, Ireland and Scotland. In the workshop you can see how coracles are made. The Centre stands on the ground floor of a 17th-century flour mill, which is also open to visitors, and there are arts, crafts, souvenirs and gifts for sale. For more information ring 01239 710980

The Old Smithy Craftshop & Heritage Centre, Cenarth Within earshot of the falls, this fascinating attraction occupies a fully-restored 18th-century blacksmith's forge which was last in operation in 1953. The Smithy's original equipment now forms part

THE OLD SMITHY CRAFTSHOP & HERITAGE CENTRE

Cenarth Falls, Newcastle Emlyn, Carms.

The Craftshop is well stocked with mainly Welsh crafts & gifts including local pottery, wood carvings, coal, slate, books, Welsh woollens, Celtic jewellery and much more.

Opening times

7 days a week – April – October
4 days a week – November & December
(Thursday – Sunday inclusive)
Open from 10.00am

Free entry to exhibition, car park and picnic area

(01239) 710067

The Wildfowler Inn

Tre'r Ddol, Machynlleth, Powys
Tel: (01970) 832 671

On the main A487 between Aberystwyth and Machynlleth

We provide an extensive inexpensive menu, including a range of home-made food, both traditional and vegetarian

• Children's Menu • Real Ale • Large Beer Garden
• Children's Play Area • Sunday Lunch

of an exhibition which also includes an interesting collection of Victorian rural antiques. Entry to the exhibition is free. The Craftshop displays a wide selection of Celtic jewellery, Welsh woollens, wood carvings, local pottery, basketware, books and many more items. The old stone cottage adjoining the craftshop and heritage centre has played an important part in Cenarth's history. Once used as the vicarage, it also served as the village school and schoolmaster's residence until a new school was built in the 1860's.

The Old Smithy Craftshop and Heritage Centre has a picnic area in the gardens, and parking is free. For more information ring 01239 710067.

Museum of the Welsh Woollen Industry This fascinating museum is 5 miles east of Newcastle Emlyn, at Drefach Felindre - the very heart of the Welsh woollen industry at the beginning of the century, with more than 40 mills working in the area. The museum is situated alongside a mill which still works today, and is housed in the buildings of what used to be the Cambrian Mills - built in 1902 and one of the biggest producers in the Teifi Valley. The museum has a collection of tools and machinery, an interpretive exhibition tracing the evolution of the industry, and a selection of contemporary designs. For more information ring 01559 370929.

North of the Dovey

The wide estuary of the River Dovey at Ynyslas marks the northern boundary of Ceredigion - but what lies beyond simply begs exploration.

Beckoning just a short distance across

King Arthur's Labyrinth

Voyage back through the mists of time by boat into huge caverns deep under the mountains where enduring tales of this ancient land unfold, bringing to life the times of King Arthur, mightiest king of the Britons.

Open daily 10am to 5pm
Visits to King Arthur's Labyrinth start from

Corris Craft Centre,
Corris, Machynlleth, Powys
Tel: 01654 761584

the sea and sand is the charming hillside resort of Aberdovey. Its superb beach, backed by sand dunes, stretches north to Tywyn. Further north still are Fairborne, Barmouth, the Lleyn Peninsula and the Snowdonia National Park.

East of Ynyslas, the wooded slopes of the Dovey Valley cut a trail to Machynlleth. Although south of the Dovey, this attractive town is the gateway to several attractions and places of interest, as described in this brief alphabetical guide.

King Arthur's Labyrinth, Corris In the darkest of the Dark Ages, the legions of the once-mighty Roman Empire had withdrawn from Britain, leaving the native Celtic peoples to defend themselves against the increasingly powerful Saxon invaders. Out of the darkness came Arthur - destined to overcome all enemies from without and within and to bring peace to these islands. His feats of bravery, supernatural powers and strength of leadership spelled defeat for the forces of darkness and, in a time when history was recorded only by word of mouth and passed on by bards and storytellers, tales of Arthur's great deeds spread throughout the land, gradually transcending the boundary between fact and legend as they were handed on from one generation to the next.

King Arthur's Labyrinth is a new attraction in Mid Wales which has captured the imagination of many visitors since opening in 1994. An underground boat takes you deep into the spectacular caverns beneath the Braichgoch mountain at Corris, near Machynlleth. As you walk through the caverns, Welsh tales of King Arthur are told with tableaux and stunning sound and light effects. The journey ends with a return trip along the beautiful subterranean river into the grounds of the Corris Craft Centre.

The Craft Centre - the starting point for King Arthur's Labyrinth - is home to six craft

AA ★★ The Wynnstay **RAC** ★★

The Friendliest Hotel in Wales

Your friendly base for a fun filled, action packed break on the edge of Spectacular Snowdonia. There's so much to do from the Wynnstay.

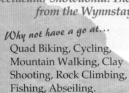

Why not have a go at...
Quad Biking, Cycling, Mountain Walking, Clay Shooting, Rock Climbing, Fishing, Abseiling.

Ideal location for...
Walking, close to links golf courses. Indoor heated pool, sauna and gymnasium adjacent to hotel.

Or visit...
Museum of Modern Art, Centre for Alternative Technology, Tabernacle Celtica Historical Centre & narrow gauge railways.

And finally...
Relax at The Wynnstay, a Georgian coaching Inn in the historic market town of Machynlleth. Sample the delights of our wonderful local produce in the restaurant, which provides a combination of traditional and modern cooking. All rooms have en-suite bathrooms. Cosy bars with real ales and fine wines.

Don't believe us...come and see for yourselves.

Wynnstay Arms Hotel, Maengwyn, Machynlleth, Powys SY20 8AE

Tel: 01654 702941 • Fax 01654 703884

YR AMGUEDDFA GYMREIG O GELFYDDYD FODERN

Y TABERNACL
THE MUSEUM OF MODERN ART, WALES

AUDITORIUM for Concerts and Conferences, in converted chapel, available for hire. Seating for 400. Modern Sound System, Projector and Screen. Multi-lingual Translation Facilities.

THE MUSEUM OF MODERN ART, WALES
YR AMGUEDDFA GYMREIG O GELFYDDYD FODERN

MONDAY - SATURDAY 10AM - 4PM ADMISSION FREE

SHOWCASE WALES - WALES' top artists and The Tabernacle Collection.
Other facilities include a Language Laboratory, Recording Studio, Dressing Rooms, Meeting Rooms and Foyer with Bar.
Auditorium and galleries accessible to a wheelchair user.

Heol Penrallt, Machynlleth SY20 8AJ.
Tel: 01654 703355. Fax: 01654 702160. email: momawales@tabernac.dircon.co.uk

workshops in which you can see first hand the skills employed in the creation of the many gift items on display. These include woodcraft, toys, jewellery, leather goods and handmade candles, and there is also a shop selling an attractive range of souvenirs, gifts and books on the Celtic Arthurian theme. The Crwybr Restaurant offers full meals, teas and refreshments throughout the day, and there is also a picnic area and children's play area.

Visitors to King Arthur's Labyrinth are advised to wear warm clothing, as the underground caverns are cool. The 45-minute tour involves a walk of about half a mile along level gravel paths which are suitable for all but the very frail. However, the variety of craft shops, gardens and refreshments within the Corris Craft Centre - plus the stunning scenery of the valley - guarantees plenty of enjoyment for everyone. For more information ring 01654 761584.

Machynlleth

Celtica Exhibition, Machynlleth A new £2.5 million attraction housed in a purpose-built extension to the former stately home of Y Plas, Machynlleth, this exciting exhibition tells the enthralling story of the Celts - past, present and future. The Celtic people emerged from the crucible of European history 3000 years ago and were heroic, inventive, resourceful and innovative. Today descendants of those early Celts still live in Wales, proud of their heritage, culture and the survival of their native Welsh language.

Celtica is a unique attraction. It was designed by John Sunderland - creator of the much-acclaimed Jorvik Viking Centre in York - and financed by Montgomeryshire District Council, assisted by the European Union. The exhibition makes very effective use of John Sunderland's highly imaginative concepts and the latest in audio-visual technology. Visitors are guided through the mystical world of Celtic roots, history and culture by two children, Nia and Gwydion - a

journey which includes a three-dimensional dramatisation of life in an early Celtic settlement, along with a visit to the Celtic 'otherworld'. There is also an interpretive centre dedicated to Welsh and Celtic history, and shops, tea rooms, creche, playground and educational facilities.

Celtica has been designed to cater for visitors with special needs, including those with hearing difficulties. There is also adequate parking. Machynlleth town centre is only a 2-minute walk away, and nearby is a leisure centre with restaurant, bar, swimming pool, flume ride, multigym and sports hall.

Dyfi Centre, Machynlleth Here you will discover displays on various aspects of local history, including slate quarrying, railways, religion, seafaring and wildlife. For more information ring 01654 702401.

Y Tabernacl, Machynlleth The Tabernacle is a former Wesleyan chapel built in 1880 and converted in 1986 as a centre for the performing arts. Linked to it is the Museum of Modern Art, Wales, which has six excellent exhibition spaces. Except for Christmas week the galleries are open daily throughout the year from 10.00am to 4.00pm, and they house two semi-permanent exhibitions - Showcase Wales, the works of Wales' top artists, and The Brotherhood of Ruralists. In addition the museum displays the Tabernacle's permanent collection and a series of temporary exhibitions. In July each year the Tabernacle Art Competition is judged by a panel of experts and selected works are exhibited throughout August. Workshops are also held and many of the works of art displayed in the museum are for sale.

The former chapel is now the auditorium for musical and theatrical performances and is also an excellent conference centre. It boasts perfect acoustics, seating up to 400 people in the old pitch-pine pews.

Translation booths, recording facilities and a cinema screen have all been installed, The Machynlleth Festival takes place in the auditorium in late August each year, featuring many eminent performers in events ranging from classical to jazz and a special concert for children. For the remainder of the year the auditorium is available for hire for performances, gatherings or conferences. Also available is the Green Room - famous for the Taliesin Mosaic adorning the walls - which is ideal for meetings, and adult classes and is equipped with a language laboratory. On Wednesdays the Tabernacle hosts a series of talks and informal performances called Midday, Market Day (12 noon - 1.00pm). For more information about the Tabernacle, ring 01654 703355. Fax 01654 702160 or e-mail:
momawales@tabernac.dircon.co.uk

Visit Europe's leading Eco-Centre

An inspiring, informative and fun day out for all ages

* Animals
* Low-energy houses
* Vegetarian restaurant
* Beautiful organic gardens
* Wind,Water and Solar Power
* Playgrounds * Book & Gift shop
* Water-powered cliff railway
* Transport Maze
* Underground "Mole-Hole" experience

CENTRE FOR ALTERNATIVE TECHNOLOGY, MACHYNLLETH SY20 9AZ.
www.cat.org.uk

Open every day. Find us on the A487, 3 miles north of Machynlleth

Tel. (01654) 702400 Fax. (01654) 702782

Centre for Alternative Technology An impressively steep funicular railway, topped by an attractive timber building, draws the eye from the main road just north of Machynlleth. This is the Centre for Alternative Technology, justly billed as a family day out with a difference.

The Centre offers an inspiring, informative and fun experience for everyone from the serious enquirer to the mildly curious. Over a period of 22 years it has established an international reputation as an educational centre where people live and work with solutions to many of the world's environmental problems.

The water-balanced cliff railway, which operates from just before Easter until the end of October, offers visitors a dramatic entrance to the 7-acre display site. Opened in 1992, the system combines solid Victorian engineering principles with modern computer control, and the view from the top is superb.

You will also be amazed at how nature has reclaimed this former slate quarry and transformed it into a truly beautiful place. The man-made water features, in particular, enhance the Centre's very special atmosphere.

Visitors explore the Centre at their own pace, most tending to follow the marked route around the various displays. These demonstrate biofuels and water, wind and solar power, with the largest electricity-producing solar roof in Britain. Energy conservation is also featured, including the

The timber building of the funicular railway

UK's best-insulated house. Most of the Centre is run on home-grown renewable electricity generated by a system independent of the national grid.

Organic growing, soil fertility, natural pest and weed control and recycling (mainly composting) are also well explained. The extensive garden areas are a rich source of ideas you can try out at home, while more ambitious visitors are drawn to the self-build display and the DIY publications. Indeed, many return for a weekend residential course.

For children there are hands-on displays to get to grips with, from the wave tank to the water and solar pumps. Then there are the animals, adventure playground and the Transport Maze. One of the biggest hits with young visitors is Megan the Mole, her underground 'Mole Hole' offering an intriguing taste of life in the soil.

The Centre's shop has a wide and unique range of books and leaflets, as well as an attractive selection of products relevant to sustainable living. The cafeteria restaurant - featured in an Egon Ronay Guide - provides many visitors with a lasting impression through tasty vegetarian lunches and refreshments.

Amazingly, the Centre for Alternative Technology is still unique in Europe. So to miss it while you are visiting this beautiful unspoilt corner of Wales would be to waste a rare opportunity indeed.

Lots of hands-on attractions

Index

A
Aberaeron 10,16
Aberarth 10,21
Aberporth 13,21
Aberystwyth 9,22
Aberystwyth Castle 24
angling 60

B
beaches, guide to 8
Borth 27

C
Cardigan 31
Cardigan Castle 31
Cardigan Island 33
Carmarthen 72
Carmarthenshire 72
Castle Henllys 69
Cei Bach 10,34
Cenarth 74
Centre for Alternative
   Technology 78
Cilborth 12
Cilgerran 35
Cilgerran Castle 35
Clarach 9,36
coracles 74
Cors Caron nature reserve
   55,57
Cors Fochno nature reserve
   28
Cwmtydu 36

D
Devil's Bridge 36
drovers 29,41
Dovey estuary 75

F
Furnace 30

G
Gilfach yr Halen 10
golf courses 60
Gwbert-on-Sea 38

H
health clubs 62
Heritage Coast 6

L
Lampeter 40
Laugharne 72
Llanbadarn Fawr 42
Llandysul 42
Llangrannog 11,45
Llanina Church 49
Llanon 47
Llanrhystud 10,45
Llansantffraid 10,47
Lochtyn Peninsula 45

M
Machynlleth 75-77
Marine Heritage Coast 6
Mwnt 13,47
Mynach Falls 37

N
National Library of Wales 67
New Quay 11,48

O
Oakwood 69
outdoor pursuits 62

P
Pembrokeshire 69
Penbryn 12,53
Pendine 72,73
Ponterwyd 53
Pontrhydfendigaid 54
pony trekking 62

R
Rheidol Valley 36

S
sailing clubs 62
Seaside Awards 8
shipbuilding 5,7
skiing 62
smuggling 5,7

soccer (Ian Rush
   tournament) 63
sports and leisure centres 63
St. David's Bishop Palace 70
St. David's Cathedral 70
St. Dogmael's 70
St. Dogmael's Abbey 70
Strata Florida Abbey 55,57
swimming pools 64

T
Tan-y-bwlch 10
Teifi, River 31
Teifi Valley Railway 73
tennis 64
Thomas, Dylan 72
Tregaron 55
Tresaith 12,59

V
Vale of Rheidol Railway 27

W
walking 66
Wallog 59
Welsh Wildlife Centre 35

Y
Ynyslas 27,30

ACKNOWLEDGEMENTS

The author's thanks are due to Centre for Alternative Technology, National Library of Wales, Ceredigion County Council, Clare & Neil Price, Andrew Lowe and the staff of Haven Colourprint, and David Lemon and all the advertisers.

Pay for 2 Persons and 1 goes FREE   Code: LILYCARDS99

TERMS & CONDITIONS.
1. Voucher cannot be used in conjunction with any other offer.
2. Pay for 2 people and 1 person goes free. Applies to entrance fee only.
3. Valid 27 March 1999 until 24 September 2000.
4. Redemption value 0.001p.
5. One voucher is required for every free entry.
6. Not valid with School groups or groups of 20 or more.
7. Voucher MUST be used by 3pm.